Node.js Web Development For Beginners

Nathan Sebhastian

Node.js Web Development For Beginners

A Step-By-Step Guide to Build an MVC Web Application With Node.js, Express, and MongoDB

By Nathan Sebhastian

https://codewithnathan.com

Table of Contents

Preface

The goal of this book is to provide gentle step-by-step instructions that will help you see how to develop web applications using Node.js, Express, and MongoDB.

I'll teach you why Node.js is a great choice to build a web application. We'll cover essential web development topics like routing, authentication, input validations, MVC design pattern, and MongoDB query to see how they are implemented in Node.js.

After finishing this book, you will know how to build and deploy a web application using Node.js.

Working Through This Book

This book is broken down into 17 concise chapters, each focusing on a specific aspect of Node.js web development. You're also going to practice what you've learned in each chapter by developing an Invoicing application.

I encourage you to write the code you see in this book and run them so that you have a sense of what web development with Node.js looks like. You learn best when you code along with examples in this book.

A tip to make the most of this book: Take at least a 10-minute break after finishing a chapter, so that you can regain your energy and focus.

Also, don't despair if some concept is hard to understand. Learning anything new is hard for the first time, especially something technical like programming. The most important thing is to keep going.

Requirements

To experience the full benefit of this book, basic knowledge of JavaScript is required.

If you need some help in learning JavaScript, you can get my book at https://codewithnathan.com/beginning-modern-javascript

Source Code

In the Summary section of each chapter, you will see a link to download the code added in that chapter from GitHub.

You can download the source code as a ZIP archive as shown below:

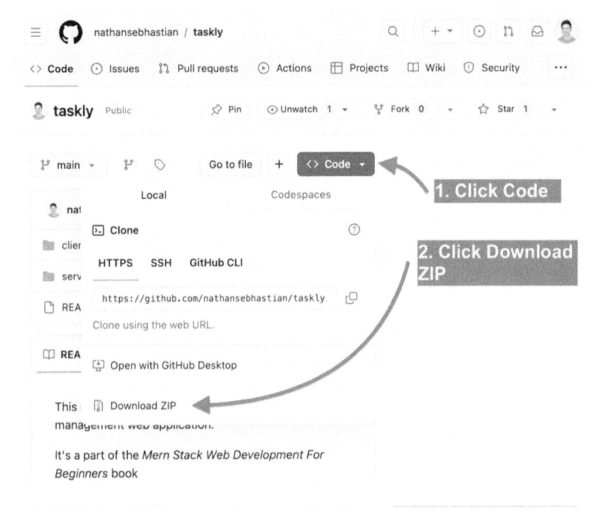

This way, you can continue to the next chapter without getting left behind.

Contact

If you need help, you can contact me at nathan@codewithnathan.com.

You might also want to subscribe to my 7-day free email course called Mindset of the Successful Software Developer at https://g.codewithnathan.com/mindset

The email course would help you find the right path forward in your career as a software developer.

Chapter 1: Introduction to Node.js

Node.js is an open-source runtime environment used for executing JavaScript code outside of the browser.

If you're familiar with JavaScript, you might know that JavaScript was first created to make the web browser programmable. JavaScript exists and runs only inside web browsers.

A complete web application is made up of two parts: the frontend or client side, and the backend or server side. The client-server architecture below shows how a web application is developed:

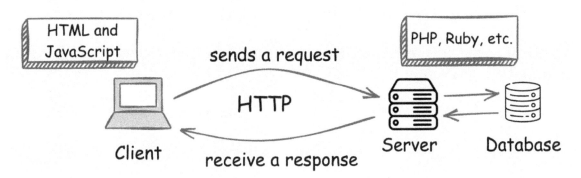

The client and server communicate using HTTP requests. When needed, a server might interact with the database to fulfill the request sent by the client.

Because JavaScript only runs in the browser, another programming language is required to build a web application. The most popular server-side programming languages are Python, Ruby, and PHP.

But all this changed with the invention of Node.js, which is a program that can run JavaScript outside of the browser.

By utilizing the power of Node.js, JavaScript can now be used to develop both the client and server side of a web application:

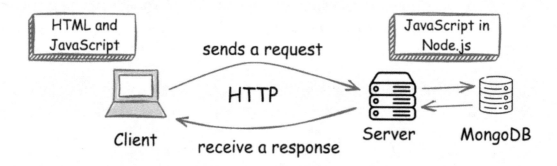

Node.js is also an extensible program, so developers have created a collection of open-source libraries and tools that simplify the web development process.

What's more, the architecture of Node.js is very flexible, which allows you to code a prototype application quickly.

In short, learning Node.js enables you to build a complete web application using just one language, which is JavaScript.

The Exercise Application

To make the learning practical, we're going to build a web application and deploy it to the public. The application we're going to build is an invoicing application.

In this application, users can add customers and invoice information:

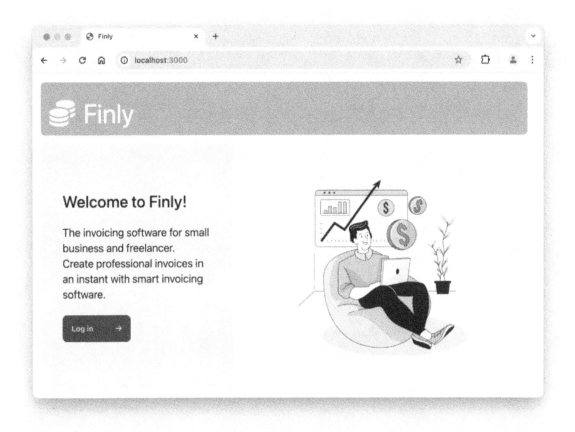

Users need to register for an account using an email and password:

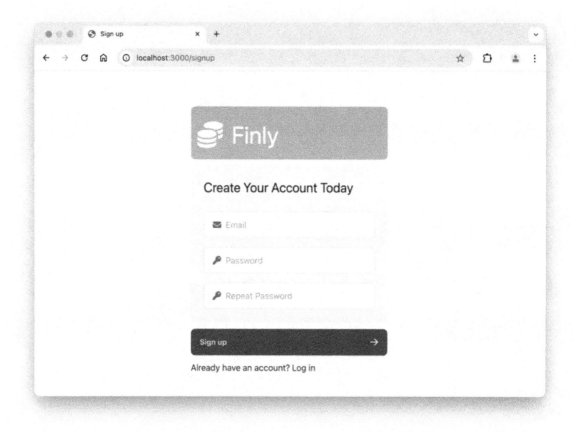

After signing up, they can add new customers to the application:

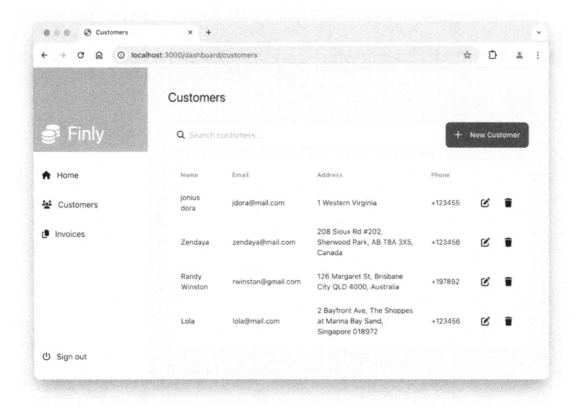

Then, users can create invoices assigned to a customer. The invoice and customer data are connected:

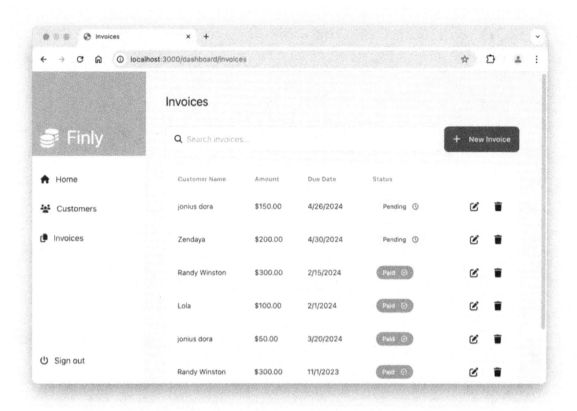

In the dashboard page, some information is shown as insights for the user. The application shows the total amount of collected and pending invoices and the number of invoices and customers created.

There's also a graph showing revenue in the last 6 months, as well as the latest invoices:

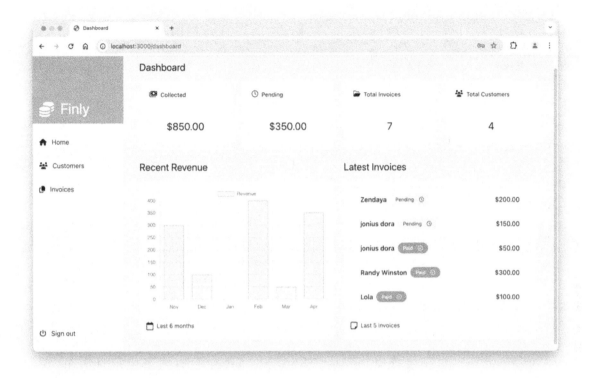

We won't include features to send the invoice by email or print it. We only focus on building the web application for storing data and showing insights.

With this practice, you will get the experience of developing a web application from scratch using Node.js, as well as understanding how to complete a project and organize your code well.

Computer Setup

To start developing with the Node.js, you need to have three things on your computer:

1. A web browser
2. A code editor
3. The Node.js program

Let's install them in the next section.

Installing Chrome Browser

Any web browser can be used to browse the Internet, but for development purposes, you need to have a browser with sufficient development tools.

The Chrome browser developed by Google is a great browser for web development, and if you don't have the browser installed, you can download it here:

https://www.google.com/chrome/

The browser is available for all major operating systems. Once the download is complete, follow the installation steps presented by the installer to have the browser on your computer.

Next, we need to install a code editor. There are several free code editors available on the Internet, such as Sublime Text, Visual Studio Code, and Notepad++.

Out of these editors, my favorite is Visual Studio Code because it's fast and easy to use.

Installing Visual Studio Code

Visual Studio Code or VSCode for short is a code editor application created for the purpose of writing code. Aside from being free, VSCode is fast and available on all major operating systems.

You can download Visual Studio Code here:

https://code.visualstudio.com/

When you open the link above, there should be a button showing the version compatible with your operating system as shown below:

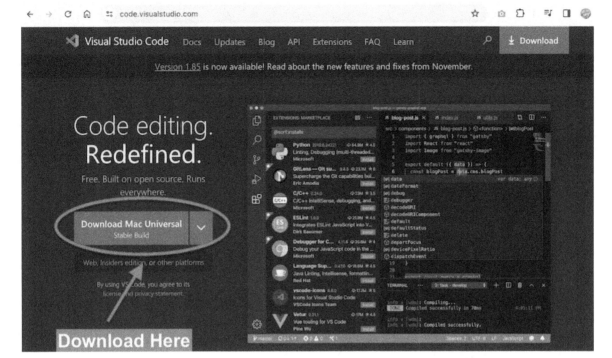

Figure 1. Install VSCode

Click the button to download VSCode, and install it on your computer.

Now that you have a code editor installed, the next step is to install Node.js

Installing Node.js

Node.js is a JavaScript runtime application that enables you to run JavaScript outside of the browser. We need this program to generate and run the web application that we're going to develop.

You can download and install Node.js from https://nodejs.org. Pick the recommended LTS version because it has long-term support. The installation process is pretty straightforward.

To check if Node has been properly installed, type the command below on your command line (Command Prompt on Windows or Terminal on Mac):

```
node -v
```

The command line should respond with the version of the Node.js you have on your computer.

You now have all the programs needed to start developing a Node.js web application. We're going to start building the application in the next chapter.

Summary

In this chapter, we've learned what is Node.js and why it's a great choice, and then we installed the required tools to develop a Node.js application.

If you encounter any issues, you can email me at nathan@codewithnathan.com and I will do my best to help you.

Chapter 2: Your First Node.js Project

Let's create a server using Node.js and implement the client-server communication that we've seen in the previous chapter.

First, create a folder on your computer that will be used to store all files and code related to this project. You can name the folder 'finly'.

Inside the folder, open your terminal and run the npm command to create a new JavaScript project:

```
npm init
```

npm stands for Node Package Manager. It's a program used for creating and installing JavaScript libraries and frameworks. It's included when you install Node.js before.

The `npm init` command is used to initialize a new project and create the `package.json` file. It will ask several questions about your project, such as the project name, version, and license.

For now, just press Enter on all questions until you see the following output:

```
About to write to /finly/package.json:

{
  "name": "finly",
  "version": "1.0.0",
  "description": "",
  "main": "index.js",
  "scripts": {
    "test": "echo \"Error: no test specified\" && exit 1"
  },
  "author": "",
  "license": "ISC"
}
```

```
Is this OK? (yes)
```

Press Enter, and you should see a `package.json` file generated in the 'finly' folder containing the same information as shown above.

Creating the Server Application

To create a Node.js server, you need to create a new file named `index.js` and write the following code in it:

```
const http = require('http');

const server = http.createServer((req, res) => {
  console.log(req.url);
  res.end('Hello From Node.js');
});

server.listen(3000, () => {
  console.log('Server running on port 3000');
});
```

In Node.js, the `require()` function is used to get a module so that you can use it. The module name is passed as an argument to the function.

The function returns the module, which you need to assign to a variable. To prevent any confusion, the imported module is usually assigned to a variable with the same name as the module.

The `http` module can then be used to create a Node.js web server by calling the `createServer()` method.

The `createServer()` method accepts a callback function, which will be executed for any incoming requests:

```
const server = http.createServer((req, res) => {
  console.log(req.url);
  res.end('Hello From Node.js');
});
```

Node.js will pass two objects to the callback function: request and response objects, or req and res for short.

The req object contains information about the network request sent by the client, while the res object is used to send a response back to the client.

In the function above, we simply log the request url value, then respond with a message 'Hello From Node.js'.

The res.end() method sends the string argument as a response and ends the request.

After that, the server.listen() method is called to open a specific web port for connections:

```
server.listen(3000, () => {
  console.log('Server running on port 3000');
});
```

The callback function will be executed when the server is running, so we call the console.log() method to let us know that the server is running.

Running the Server

To run the server, open the terminal and run the JavaScript file using Node.js as follows:

```
node index.js
```

You should see 'Server listening at port 3000' logged to the terminal.

Now you can open the browser and visit the website at http://localhost:3000 to get the following response:

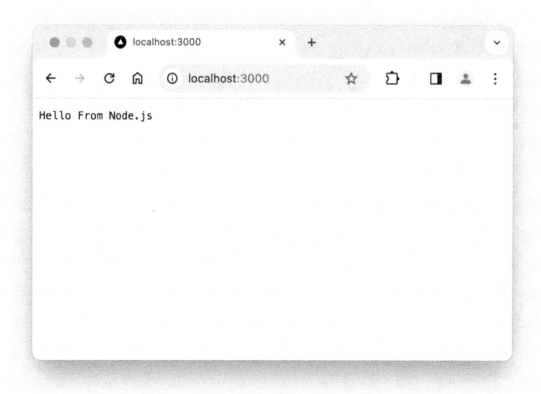

You now have a working server, and you can send a request to that server from the client (browser). Nice work!

Routing in Node.js

Now that the web server is created, let's add some routes to the server so that it can have different responses.

A route is a specific URL address that points to a specific response. It's like a map that the web server uses to know what to do with incoming requests.

In the previous section, we logged the `req.url` value to the terminal for each incoming request.

If you try to navigate to different routes such as localhost:3000/about or localhost:3000/contact, you'll see the URL logged as follows:

```
/
/about
/contact
```

This means we already have the means to detect the URL. We only need to make use of this data to change the response.

To add routes to the server, you can use an `if` statement to check for the `req.url` value, and send the desired response like this:

```javascript
const server = http.createServer((req, res) => {
  const { url } = req;
  console.log(url);
  if(url === '/') {
    res.end('Hello From Node.js');
  } else if (url === '/contact') {
    res.end('The Contact Page');
  } else if (url === '/about') {
    res.end('The About Page');
  } else {
    res.writeHead(404)
    res.end('Not Found');
  }
});
```

First, we unpack the `url` value from the `req` object, so we don't have to write `req.url` every time we want to access the URL value.

After logging the `url` value. We create an `if-else` statement to define different responses for the request.

When the `url` route is not defined, we send back `404` error code.

The `writeHead()` method allows you to write specific data that you want to send back to the client. The default response code `200` means the request is processed correctly, while `404` indicates a 'Not Found' error.

The code you added to the `index.js` file won't take effect immediately.

You need to stop the server by pressing `Control + C` on the terminal, then run `node index.js` again for the changes to work.

Now if you visit different routes on the localhost, you'll see different responses because of the routing that you've implemented.

Adding Nodemon for Development

Notice that after changing and saving the `index.js` file, you need to restart the Node server for the changes to work.

You're going to add more code to this project in the following chapters, and if you still use `node`, then you have to do the restart every time you make some changes.

To make the development more pleasing, let's use Nodemon to run the server instead.

Nodemon is a monitoring script that will automatically restart Node.js when it detects any changes to the files in your project.

To use Nodemon, You need to install it using npm first:

```
npm install nodemon --save-dev
```

The `--save-dev` option is used to specify packages that are only needed for development purposes.

Packages marked as dev dependencies won't be installed when you deploy the application to a production environment later.

If you open the package.json file, you should see nodemon listed as devDependencies like this:

```
"devDependencies": {
  "nodemon": "^3.1.0"
}
```

You will also have package-lock.json file and node_modules/ folder generated on the project.

The package-lock.json file is used to record the exact version of the packages you installed. It's only useful when you need to upgrade or downgrade installed packages.

The node_modules/ folder is where the packages you install using npm will be stored.

After installing Nodemon, add a start and dev script on the package.json file as shown below:

```
"scripts": {
  "start": "node index.js",
  "dev": "nodemon index.js"
}
```

The scripts in package.json file respond to the npm run <script-name> command that you can run from the terminal.

To run the dev script, run the npm run dev command.

Nodemon will execute the index.js file and show the following output:

```
npm run dev

> finly@1.0.0 dev
> nodemon index.js

[nodemon] 3.1.0
[nodemon] to restart at any time, enter `rs`
[nodemon] watching path(s): *.*
[nodemon] watching extensions: js,mjs,cjs,json
[nodemon] starting `node index.js`
Server listening at port 3000
```

To see Nodemon in action, open the index.js file and change the message returned by the / route as follows:

```
if(url === '/') {
  res.end('Hello World!');
}
```

You will see Nodemon automatically restart the server in the terminal as follows:

```
[nodemon] restarting due to changes...
[nodemon] starting `node index.js`
Server listening at port 3000
```

Now change the message back to 'Hello From Node.js', and you'll see the restart message again on the terminal.

If you don't use Nodemon, then you'll have to restart the server manually when you make changes to the project. Thank you Nodemon!

Summary

The code added in this chapter can be found at https://g.codewithnathan.com/node-2

You've managed to create your first Node.js server and implemented routes that respond to specific URL requests.

You've also installed Nodemon so that the server automatically restarts whenever you add any changes to the project.

In the next chapter, we're going to learn about Express, the web application framework for Node.js.

Chapter 3: Introduction to Express and Morgan

Using the `http` module, you've created a server that can receive HTTP requests.

But as you can see from the routing implementation, building a web application using Node.js is verbose and complicated.

To simplify the process of building a web application, you can use a framework called Express.

Express is a Node.js web framework that's popular because of its simplicity and minimalist nature. The framework is built on top of Node.js modules like `http`.

By using Express, you gain access to functions and modules that speed up the development process. Let me show you an example.

Using Express

To start using Express, you need to install the package using npm as follows:

```
npm install express
```

Once the package is installed, open the `index.js` file and replace the `http` server you've created before with this:

```
const express = require('express');

const app = express();

app.get('/', (req, res) => {
  res.send('Hello From Node.js');
```

```
});

app.get('/contact', (req, res) => {
  res.send('The Contact Page');
});

app.get('/about', (req, res) => {
  res.send('The About Page');
});

const PORT = 3000;

app.listen(PORT, () => {
  console.log(`Server running on port ${PORT}`);
});
```

Here, we import the express module and call the express() function to create an Express application.

This application will be a server that responds to network requests.

From this application, you can write the same routes created using http module before:

```
app.get('/', (req, res) => {
  res.send('Hello From Node.js');
});

app.get('/contact', (req, res) => {
  res.send('The Contact Page');
});

app.get('/about', (req, res) => {
  res.send('The About Page');
});
```

Instead of using an if-else statement, Express enables you to specify and separate the URL routes available in your application.

The `app.get()` method is used to respond to GET HTTP requests. If you want to specify a route for the POST method, you can use `app.post()` instead (more on this later as we build the application)

After that, you can call the `app.listen()` method to enable the server to listen for requests. We add the port number as a constant just to make it reusable.

To add a Not Found 404 page, you can add another `app.get()` method above the `PORT` variable as follows:

```
app.get('*', (req, res) => {
  res.status(404).send('Not Found');
});

const PORT = 3000;
```

The asterisk * symbol is known as the wild card route, and it will match any URL route.

Because the route matches any URL such as `localhost:3000/a` and `localhost:3000/b`, you need to define this route at the bottom of your routes.

The ordering of the routes matters in Express. If you place the asterisk route on top of other routes like this:

```
app.get('*', (req, res) => {
  res.status(404).send('Not Found');
});

app.get('/', (req, res) => {
  res.send('Hello From Node.js');
});

app.get('/contact', (req, res) => {
  res.send('The Contact Page');
});
```

Then you'll get the 404 response even when you visit a valid. Make sure that you define a wild card route as the last route on your application.

Adding Morgan for Logging

One thing you might notice is that we no longer log the URL request to the terminal.

Because Express separates the request handlers into their own get() methods, logging the URL means you need to write a console.log on each handler like this:

```
app.get('/', (req, res) => {
  console.log(req.url);
  res.send('Hello From Node.js');
});

app.get('/contact', (req, res) => {
  console.log(req.url);
  res.send('The Contact Page');
});
```

That doesn't look very good! Instead of logging the URL manually, let's use Morgan to create a detailed log instead.

Morgan is a library that you can use to report detailed logs for your Node.js application.

To use this library, you need to install it using npm first:

```
npm install morgan
```

Then in your index.js file, import the module and call the app.use() method as follows:

```
const express = require('express');
const morgan = require('morgan');
```

```
const app = express();

app.use(morgan('dev'));
```

The `app.use()` method is used to register a middleware function so that it will be executed on each request.

Here, we call the `morgan()` function and pass the format we want to use for the logs, which is 'dev'.

There are other formats such as 'tiny' and 'common' that you can use, but 'dev' is the best for development use.

I will explain what a middleware does later. For now, let's run the server and try to visit some of the available routes.

You'll see logs created by Morgan as follows:

```
GET / 304 5.390 ms - -
GET /about 304 0.654 ms - -
GET /contact 304 0.671 ms - -
```

Here, you can see that Morgan logs the request method, the URL route, the status returned by the server, and the amount of time required to send a response back in milliseconds.

By using Morgan, the logs will be more useful as you develop the application.

Summary

The code added in this chapter can be found at https://g.codewithnathan.com/node-3

In this chapter, you've learned how Express makes the web development process more convenient.

You can separate the route handlers by using Express `get()` methods, so you don't need to create nested if statements.

You've also learned about the Morgan library, which is used for creating detailed logs.

Chapter 4: Using EJS Templating Engine for Views

Using route handlers isn't the only benefit of using Express.

The framework also includes templating engines that you can use to create and send responses to the client.

Instead of sending back static HTML pages, templating engines allow you to dynamically render your HTML pages.

Let me show you how templating engines work in the next section

Adding EJS to Express

There are many templating engines that are compatible with Express, such as Pug, Handlebars, and EJS.

These templating engines have different syntaxes, but they all serve the same purpose: to create HTML output from the provided data.

We're going to use EJS for our application because it uses plain JavaScript, so the syntax will be familiar and easy to understand.

To use EJS, install the package using npm:

```
npm install ejs
```

Next, open the index.js file, and set the view engine for Express as follows:

```
const app = express();
```

```
app.set('views', './views');
app.set('view engine', 'ejs');
```

The `app.set()` method is used to add specific configurations to Express. Here, we set the 'views' option to the `./views` folder.

Next, create the `views/` folder in our project, create a new file named `index.ejs`, and add the following code:

```
<!DOCTYPE html>
<html lang="en">
<head>
  <meta charset="UTF-8">
  <meta name="viewport" content="width=device-width, initial-scale=1.0">
  <title>Document</title>
</head>
<body>
  <h1><%= message %></h1>
  <p>Response created using EJS</p>
</body>
</html>
```

Notice that EJS file contains plain HTML code except for the `<%= message %>` tag.

Ejs enables you to embed JavaScript by using the `<% %>` tag. Inside this tag, you can write JavaScript code such as declaring a variable or adding an `if` statement.

In the code above, we simply output the content of the `message` variable, which we're going to add next.

Rendering EJS Template With Express

To render EJS template, you need to use the `res.render()` method provided by the `res` object, and specify the `.ejs` file you want to render.

Go back to your `index.js` file and change the response inside the route handlers as follows:

```
app.get('/', (req, res) => {
  res.render('index', { message: 'Hello From Node.js' });
});

app.get('/contact', (req, res) => {
  res.render('index', { message: 'The Contact Page' });
});

app.get('/about', (req, res) => {
  res.render('index', { message: 'The About Page' });
});

app.get('*', (req, res) => {
  res.status(404).render('index', { message: 'Not Found' });
});
```

Here, the render() method accepts 2 arguments.

The first argument is the EJS template to render, which is the index file. You can omit the .ejs extension as shown above.

The second argument is an object containing options you want to send to the template. The object properties are available in EJS as variables.

In the code above, we specify the message property so that EJS can render the output.

Now run the server and visit the website routes. You'll see the HTML response as follows:

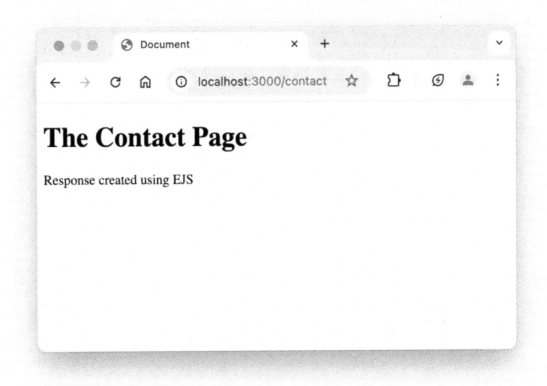

By using EJS, you can use one template file to produce HTML output with different content. It allows you to reuse the same layout for multiple pages.

What's more, you can also avoid repetitive code by creating partial templates. Let me show you how.

Reuse EJS Template With Partials

Inside the `views/` folder, create a folder named `partials`, then create an EJS file named `head.ejs` and add the `<head>` tag in this file:

```
<head>
  <meta charset="UTF-8">
  <meta name="viewport" content="width=device-width, initial-scale=1.0">
```

```
    <title>Document</title>
  </head>
```

Now you can reuse this template in any other EJS template by using the `include()` function.

Back on the `index.ejs` file, replace the `<head>` tag with the following code:

```
<!DOCTYPE html>
<html lang="en">
<%- include('./partials/head') %>
<!-- body tag... -->
</html>
```

Now whenever you create another EJS template, you can use the `include()` function to reuse a certain part of the template.

This will be useful as you develop the application features later.

Summary

The code added in this chapter can be found at https://g.codewithnathan.com/node-4

Aside from helping you create a cleaner and more manageable codebase, using Express also enables you to use JavaScript templating engines.

Using a JavaScript templating engine like EJS enables you to programmatically change the output produced by Express routes.

You can define the layout using HTML, while changing the data shown by Express using JavaScript variables, statements, and methods.

You'll see the power of EJS more in the coming chapters.

Chapter 5: Using Tailwind and DaisyUI for CSS

Now that we can create the interface of our application using EJS, let's add CSS libraries so we can speed up the development process.

For styling the interface, we're going to use Tailwind CSS and Daisy UI.

If you aren't familiar with Tailwind CSS, it's basically a collection of CSS classes where each class applies minimal styling to the element.

CSS frameworks like Bootstrap and Bulma provide you with high-level components that you can immediately use in your project.

When you need to style a button, you just need to apply the classes that contain the desired CSS properties:

```
<button className="btn btn-primary">Subscribe</button>
```

When using Bootstrap, the `btn` class provides a combination of CSS properties such as padding, color, opacity, font weight, and so on.

On the other hand, Tailwind gives you utility classes where each class has only one or two properties:

```
<button className='px-5 py-2 text-white bg-blue-500 border-2'>
  Subscribe
</button>
```

In the example above, the `px-5` is short for padding `padding-left` and `padding-right`, while 5 is a specific size for the paddings. The `text-white` applies `color: white`, the `bg-blue-500` applies the `background-color` property, and `border` applies `border-width`.

By using Tailwind, you get the flexibility of applying styles to your element by adding the desired class.

But since Tailwind doesn't come with pre-made components, we need to specify a bunch of CSS classes just to create common components like a button, a dropdown, and a navigation bar.

To avoid building components from scratch, we're also going to add DaisyUI to the application. Let's do it!

Adding Tailwind CSS to Node.js Project

To use Tailwind in a Node.js application, you need to install the required packages first using npm.

From the terminal, run the following command:

```
npm install --save-dev tailwindcss postcss autoprefixer postcss-cli
```

After installing the dependencies, you need to initialize Tailwind CSS configuration by running the `tailwindcss init` command:

```
npx tailwindcss init -p
```

Tailwind will generate two files in your project: the `tailwind.config.js` and `postcss.config.js` files.

The `tailwind.config.js` file is used to configure Tailwind. You can define where to find the HTML files, JavaScript components, or any other template files to scan here.

Open the `tailwind.config.js` file and fill the `content` parameter with the location of your view files:

```
/** @type {import('tailwindcss').Config} */
export default {
  content: ['./views/**/*.ejs'],
  theme: {
    extend: {},
  },
  plugins: [],
}
```

The `postcss.config.js` file is used to configure PostCSS, which is the tool used to run CSS compilation. There's no change you need to make in this file.

Next, create a new folder named `public/`, then create a new folder named `styles/` in it, then create a `tailwind.css` file with the following content:

```
/* tailwind.css */
@tailwind base;
@tailwind components;
@tailwind utilities;
```

This file needs to be processed by PostCSS.

In your `package.json` file, add the script command `devcss` to run PostCSS and produce a CSS file containing Tailwind styles:

```
{
  "dev": "nodemon index.js",
  "devcss": "postcss public/styles/tailwind.css -o public/styles/style.css -w"
}
```

The `-o` option is used to tell PostCSS where to put the produced CSS file. In our case, it's `public/styles/style.css`.

The `-w` option passed to PostCSS will make it watch our template files for any changes, and then run the process again.

You are now ready to use Tailwind in your application. Open the `index.ejs` file and create a simple heading component to test this:

```
<html lang="en">
<%- include('./partials/head') %>
<body>
  <h1 class="text-3xl font-bold text-teal-500">
    <%= message %>
  </h1>
</body>
</html>
```

Also, make sure you add the generated CSS file in your template. Add the link to the generated `.css` file in your `views/partials/head.ejs` file:

```
<head>
  <meta charset="UTF-8">
  <meta name="viewport" content="width=device-width, initial-scale=1.0">
  <title>Document</title>
  <link href="/styles/style.css" rel="stylesheet" />
</head>
```

Now we need to make the `public/` folder static so that the browser can reach the `style.css` file.

In your `index.js` file, call the `app.use()` method and pass `express.static()` as its argument:

```
app.use(morgan('dev'));
app.use(express.static('./public'));
```

Now run the CSS process from the terminal:

```
npm run devcss
```

If you open the `style.css` file, you should see styles generated by PostCSS and Tailwind.

Open the browser and you should see the `<h1>` element styled with Tailwind styles:

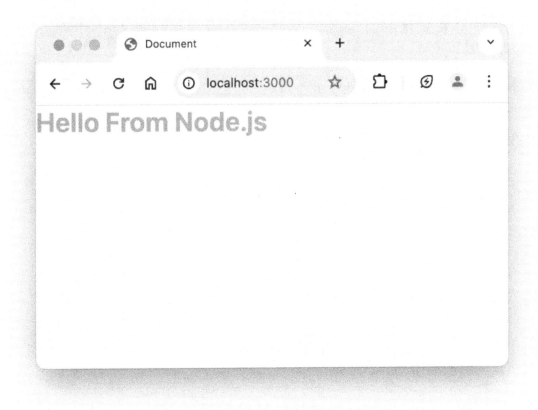

Looking good! We're going to add DaisyUI on top of Tailwind next.

Using DaisyUI

DaisyUI is a CSS component library that uses Tailwind CSS under the hood. The library provides CSS classes that you can use to create common components like a button, a form input, a dropdown, and so on.

To add DaisyUI to the application, you need to install the package using npm like this:

```
npm install --save-dev daisyui
```

Once the installation is finished, you can add DaisyUI on top of the Tailwind module you added earlier.

Open the `tailwind.config.js` file and add `require('daisyui')` to the `plugins` config as follows:

```
/** @type {import('tailwindcss').Config} */
module.exports = {
  content: [
    // ...
  ],
  theme: {
    // ...
  },
  plugins: [require('daisyui')],
};
```

With that, you can use DaisyUI class names in your application.

To test this, let's create a button in the `index.ejs` file like this:

```
<body>
  <h1 class="text-emerald-500"><%= message %></h1>
  <p class="text-emerald-800">Response created using EJS</p>
  <button class="btn btn-primary m-2">Click me!</button>
</body>
```

Go back to the browser, and refresh the page to see a button rendered as follows:

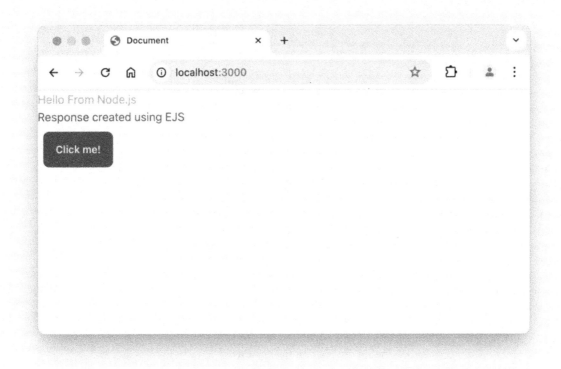

Notice that when creating the button, we also add the `m-2` class to add margins around the button.

This is a base class from the Tailwind library, and it can be used together with classes from DaisyUI anytime you need it.

This is why I love using Tailwind. I can use pre-made components to build the interface for my application, and whenever I want to customize the component, I just add Tailwind classes to the element.

You can also pair Tailwind with Bootstrap, but the integration is more complex than pairing Tailwind with DaisyUI.

Summary

If you need to check the code added in this chapter, you can visit the GitHub repo at https://g.codewithnathan.com/node-5

In this chapter, we've integrated Tailwind and DaisyUI so that we can build the view layer faster.

Chapter 6: Creating a MongoDB Database Cluster

When developing a web application, a database is essential for storing and managing information that's important for the application.

In this chapter, you're going to learn about the MongoDB database software and how to create one for free.

Don't worry if you never used MongoDB before. I'll introduce how the database works in a nutshell and guide you through creating the database.

MongoDB Introduction

If you already know about MongoDB, you can fast forward to 'Setting Up MongoDB Atlas Cloud' section below.

MongoDB is one of many databases that you can use to store web application data. It's a document-oriented database that provides flexible and scalable solutions for storing and retrieving data.

MongoDB is also known as a NoSQL database because it doesn't use the Structured Query Language (SQL) for accessing and manipulating the stored data.

Some of the most popular SQL databases are MySQL, SQLite, and PostgreSQL. You might have heard or used them before.

In an SQL database, data is stored under tables and rows. Suppose we want to use the database to keep track of users and events that are created in our application.

Here's a representation of the data in an SQL database:

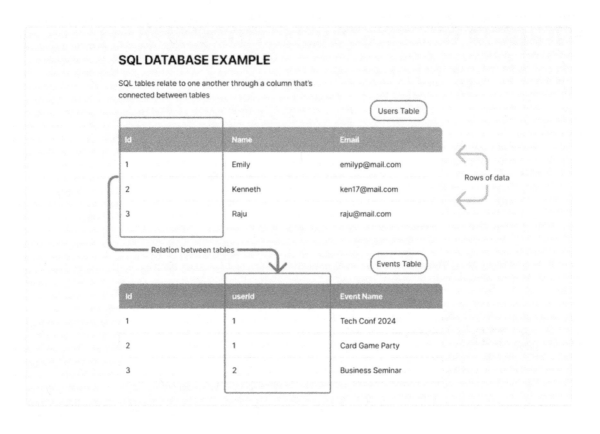

SQL DATABASE EXAMPLE

SQL tables relate to one another through a column that's connected between tables

Users Table

Id	Name	Email
1	Emily	emilyp@mail.com
2	Kenneth	ken17@mail.com
3	Raju	raju@mail.com

Rows of data

Relation between tables

Events Table

Id	userId	Event Name
1	1	Tech Conf 2024
2	1	Card Game Party
3	2	Business Seminar

In the above example, the Users Table and the Events Table represent the users and events data respectively.

In each table, there are rows of data, and the Id column in the Users Table is related to the userId column in the Events Table.

Through the relation created in these tables, we can see that the first two events were created by the user 'Emily', while the third one was created by 'Kenneth'.

When you update the Id value in the Users Table, the userId value in the Events Table will be updated automatically.

By contrast, a NoSQL database like MongoDB represents the data as documents and collections.

A collection can have many documents, and each document can have as many entries of data. A document can store a reference to another document:

NOSQL DATABASE EXAMPLE

noSQL database stores data in collections and documents.
A document relate to another document by **references**
stored in the document

Users Collection		
Id: 1, Name: Emily, Email: emilyp@mail.com	Id: 2, Name: Kenneth, Email: ken17@mail.com	Id: 3, Name: Raju, Email: raju@mail.com

Events Collection		
Id: 1, userId: 1, Event Name: 'Tech Conf 2024'	Id: 2, userId: 1, Event Name: 'Card Game Party'	Id: 3, userId: 2, Event Name: 'Business Seminar'

Since a NoSQL database is non-relational, the `userId` entry in the Events Collection won't be updated automatically when you update the `Id` entry in the Users Collection.

There are many articles available about the comparisons between NoSQL and SQL databases, but this will be enough for now.

Let's continue with setting up a MongoDB instance for our application to use next.

Setting Up MongoDB Atlas Cloud

The easiest and quickest way to get started with MongoDB is to sign up for its cloud service, which is MongoDB Atlas.

When using MongoDB Atlas, you don't need to manually install and run MongoDB on your computer for development and testing. The cloud service will generate a server instance for MongoDB along with credentials to access the database.

MongoDB Atlas also has a free tier which is perfect for our Express server project, so head over to https://www.mongodb.com/atlas/database and click on the 'Try Free' button shown on the page:

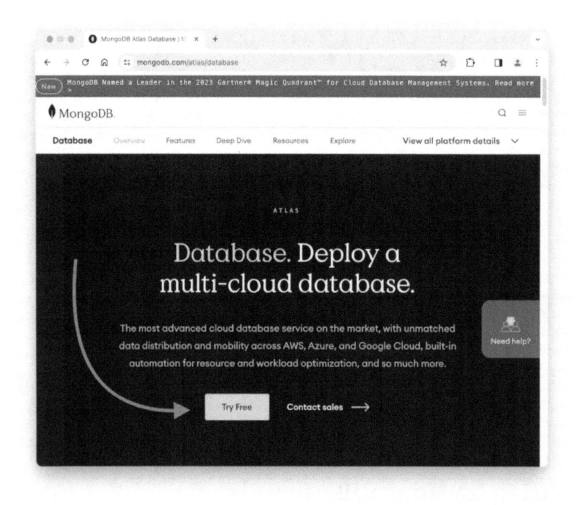

You'll be taken to the registration page, where you can create an account for free:

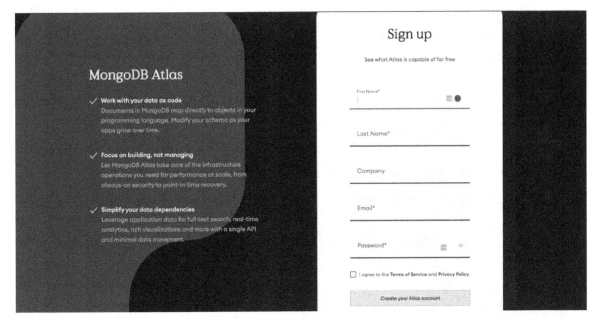

Figure 2. MongoDB Atlas Sign Up Page

1. Fill in the required fields.

2. When you're done, click "Create your Atlas account".

3. Next, you will be sent an email verification. Verify your email by clicking the "Verify Email" button on that email as shown in the image below:

Figure 3. MongoDB Atlas Verify Email

1. After verifying your email, head back to the [Login page](https://account.mongodb.com/account/login) and login using your credentials.

Welcome to Atlas

Upon logging in for the first time, you will be presented with a "Welcome to Atlas!" page.

1. For "What is your goal primary goal?", select "Learn MongoDB".

2. For "How long have you been developing software with MongoDB??", select "Less than a year".

3. Select "JavaScript / Node.js" as your primary language.

4. For "What kind(s) of data will your project use?" and "Will your application include any of the following architectural models?", you can select any answer. Select "Not sure/None" if you want to skip these.

Your form should look like the image below:

Atlas

Welcome to Atlas. Let's build something great.

Help us tailor your experience by taking a minute to answer the questions below.

GETTING TO KNOW YOU

What is your primary goal?

| Learn MongoDB | ▾ |

How long have you been developing software with MongoDB?

| Less than a year | ▾ |

GETTING TO KNOW YOUR PROJECT

What programming language are you primarily building on MongoDB with?

| JavaScript / Node.js | ▾ |

What kind(s) of data will your project use?

You can choose as many as you want

| Customer... ✖ | ⊗ ▾ |

Will your application include any of the following architectural models?

You can choose as many as you want

| Not sure... ✖ | ⊗ ▾ |

Finish

Figure 4. MongoDB Atlas Welcome Form

Create a Cluster

Upon completing the form, you will be directed to the *Deploy your database* page.

If you arrive at the Overview page instead, you can click the big green + *Create* button to go to the *Deploy your database* page:

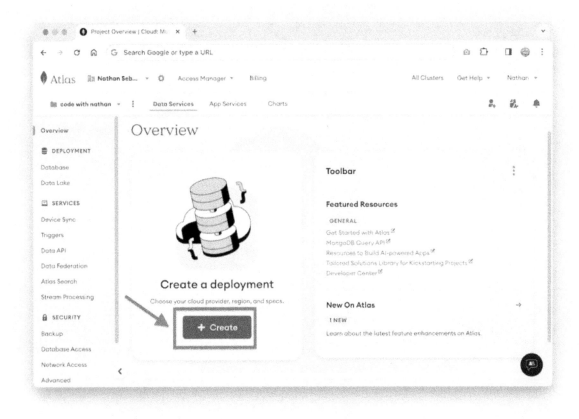

Figure 5. MongoDB Atlas Overview Page

On the *Deploy your database* page, Select the *M0 FREE* plan, which is ideal for testing and development:

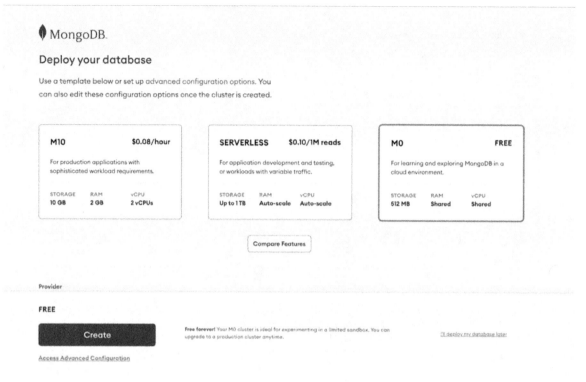

Figure 6. MongoDB Atlas Plans

The *Provider* option is the cloud service provider that will host your database. You're free to select whichever you like.

AWS, Google Cloud, and Azure all offer the same free tier. For the region, select the region that's recommended or is closest to you.

You can accept the default cluster name provided, usually 'Cluster0'. Leave the tag empty as it's optional. After selecting your provider and nearest region, you can click the green "Create" button:

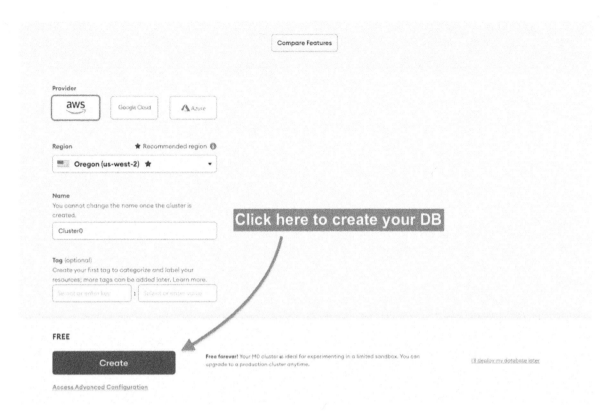

Figure 7. MongoDB Atlas Create Database

Now you need to wait a bit for the cluster to be created by MongoDB. If this is the first time you use MongoDB Atlas, you'll be taken directly to the *Security Quickstart* page after the cluster is created.

Security Quickstart: Set Authentication and Connection

Here, you'll be asked two questions. First is how to authenticate connections to your database.

You can select Username and Password, then use the Username and Password that have been generated for you. Click *Create User* as shown below:

Security Quickstart

To access data stored in Atlas, you'll need to create users and set up network security controls. Learn more about security set

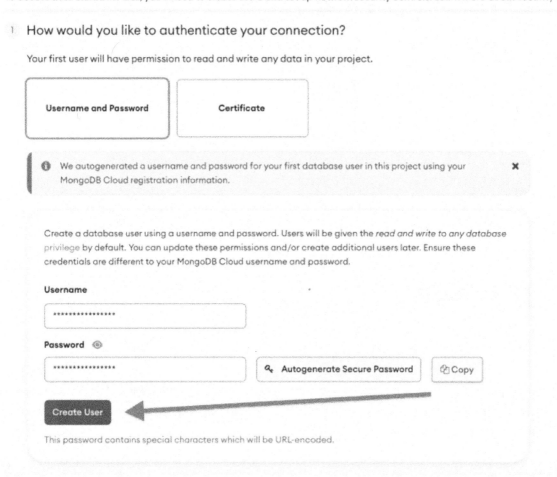

Next, you need to enable access to the database from specific IP addresses. Because this is a development database, you can enter '0.0.0.0' as the IP address value to enable access from anywhere:

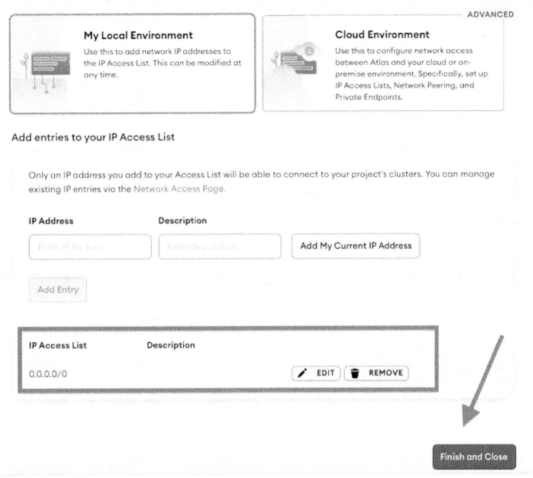

Now you can click *Finish and Close*. You should be redirected to the *Overview* page, where your active cluster is shown:

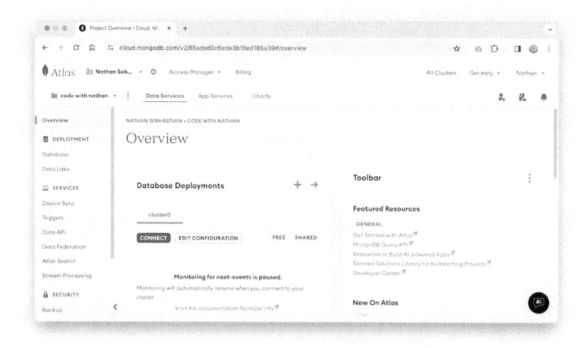

The cluster is ready to accept incoming connections. Great work!

Add a New Database User

There may be times when you want to add another user or whitelist an IP address. Because the *Security Quickstart* is gone after you create a cluster, you need to navigate the Atlas menu.

To add a new database user, follow these steps:

1. On the left-hand navigation menu, under Security, select the *Database Access* link.

2. From there, click the *Add New Database User* button just above the Users table. The following image shows the create user modal with the options you'll need to select:

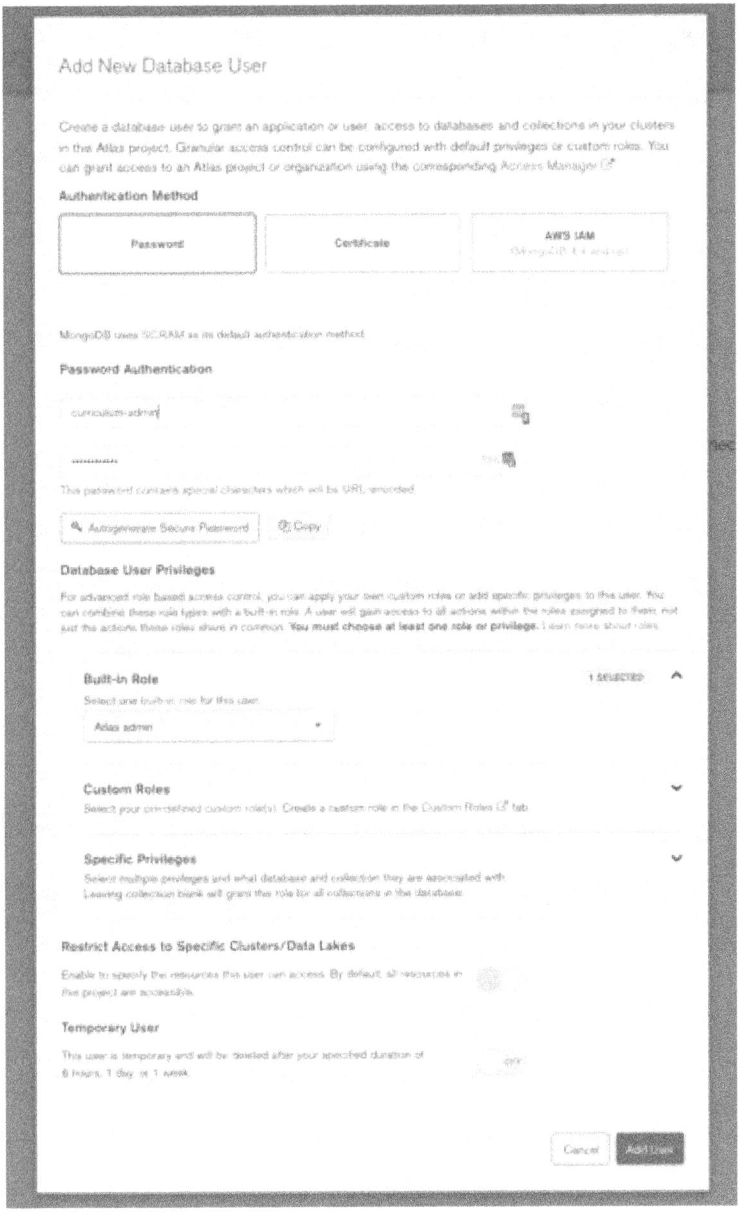

Figure 8. Adding a New User to Database

To fill out the form, follow these steps:

- For *Authentication Method*, choose *Password*.

- Under *Password Authentication*, create a Username and Password that you'll remember.

- Under *Database User Privileges*, select *Atlas admin*.

- Leave any remaining options as default.

- IMPORTANT: Do not enable *Temporary User* unless you want to make a new user every so often.

- When you're done, click *Add User*.

Allow Your IP Address

To allow a new IP address, you need to select the *Network Access* menu from the *Security* tab on the left side, then add the IP address you want.

On the Network Access page, click the *Add IP Address* green button and a modal will appear:

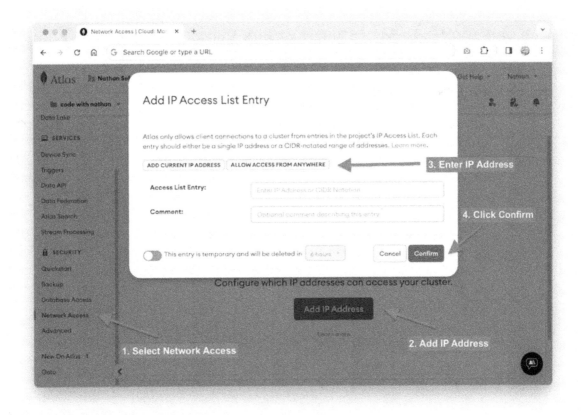

Figure 9. Whitelisting an IP Address

You can add your IP address in the modal shown above. You can also enable connection from anywhere by clicking the *Allow Access From Anywhere* button, or just add your IP address with the *Add Current IP Address* button.

Click *Confirm* when you're done, and that's how you add a new user or IP address in MongoDB Atlas.

With your database cluster ready, it's time to try connecting your Express application to the database.

Summary

Note that there's no code repository for this chapter because we didn't add any.

In this chapter, we've learned what is MongoDB database, the difference between MongoDB and SQL databases, and how to set up a MongoDB Atlas cluster for free.

A MongoDB cluster can have many databases, although you usually only need one database for a single application.

In the next chapter, we're going to see how to connect the MongoDB cluster to our Node application.

Chapter 7: Integrating Mongoose to Express

Now that we've created a MongoDB cluster, it's time to enable Express to connect to the database.

To do so, we need to use a library called Mongoose. Let's get started.

Mongoose Introduction

Mongoose is an Object Data Modeling (ODM) library for MongoDB and Node.js. This library can be used to define relationships between data, provide schema validation, and send queries to your MongoDB database.

As a database, MongoDB doesn't provide a schema where you can describe the data structure of your documents. This means the data you put in a document is unrestricted.

You can put different types of data in the same field like this:

```
{
  "Id": 1,
  "name": "Emily",
},
{
  "Id": "2",
  "name": "John",
  "age": 28,
}
```

If you look closely, the Id field in the first document is a number, but it's a string in the second document.

What's more, the second document contains an age field, which is not present in the first document. This database is messy because it has no structure.

By using Mongoose, you can create a schema that defines the shape of your data. The schema can be written in JavaScript like this:

```
const UserSchema = new Schema({
  name: { type: String, required: true },
  age: { type: Number, required: false },
})
```

The schema is an object that defines the characteristics of your data document, such as:

- What value type does the field accept?
- Is the data required (can't be empty)?
- Does it have to be unique (no duplicate in the collection)?

Technically, the Mongoose library acts as a 'bridge' between our Express application and the MongoDB cluster.

While you can connect to MongoDB without Mongoose, using the library is recommended because you can validate your data before inserting it into the database.

The library is also free, so you only need to install it using npm.

As always, I will hold your hand through installing and using Mongoose.

Connecting to MongoDB Cluster

Let's use Mongoose to connect to the MongoDB cluster we've created in the previous chapter.

First, you need to install mongoose and mongodb in your Node.js application using npm:

```
npm install mongodb mongoose
```

Next, create a file named `dbConnect.js` in your `lib/` folder and write the following code in it:

```
const mongoose = require('mongoose');

const MONGODB_URI = process.env.MONGODB_URI;

if (!MONGODB_URI) throw new Error('MONGODB_URI is missing');

mongoose.connect(MONGODB_URI, {
  dbName: 'finly-db',
  bufferCommands: false,
});

console.log('Connected to MongoDB');
```

This code is used to open a connection to the MongoDB cluster.

When we call the `mongoose.connect()` method, Mongoose will try to connect to the MongoDB cluster URI that we specify as `MONGODB_URI`.

The `dbName` argument provides the name of the database you want to connect to. If it doesn't exist, Mongoose will create one on the cluster.

The `bufferCommands` option is set to `false` to disable buffering. This makes sure that a connection exists before you send further instructions to manipulate the database.

When you're connected to the cluster, you'll see a 'Connected to MongoDB' log on the terminal.

Next, look at how the connection requires an environment variable named `MONGODB_URI` for the connection:

```
const MONGODB_URI = process.env.MONGODB_URI;
```

To get this URI, you need to go back to MongoDB Atlas Overview page, and click the *Connect* button on your cluster card:

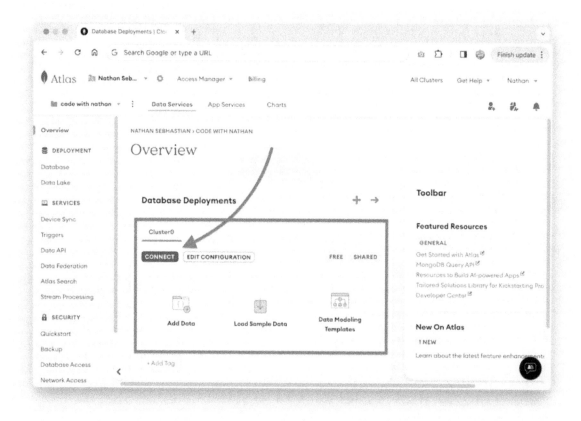

Figure 10. Click the Connect button in MongoDB Cluster

You will see a tab where you can choose the connection method. Choose *Driver* as shown below:

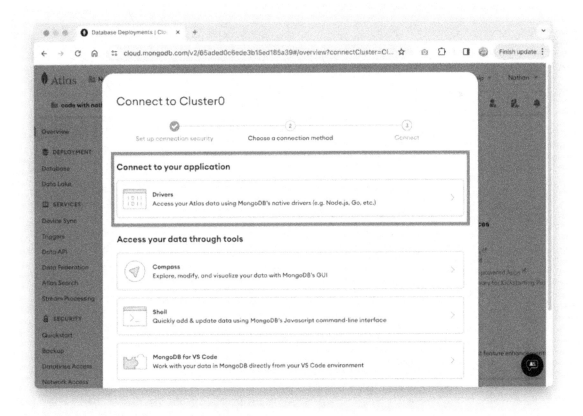

You'll be shown the connection string URI on the next page as shown below:

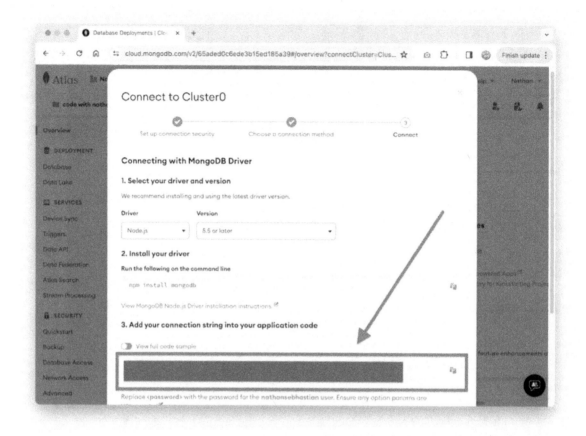

Copy the connection string, then create a `.env` file in your application root folder with the following content:

```
MONGODB_URI=<Paste your connection string here>
```

Note that you also need to replace the `<password>` string in the URI with your user's password.

If you forgot the password, you need to create a new password by selecting *Database Access* and editing the password of the user you created earlier.

Installing Dotenv to Read Environment Variables

Both Node.js and Express won't load the environment variables by default.

To enable the environment variables, you need to install a node package called dotenv first:

```
npm install dotenv
```

Once the package is installed, open the index.js file and call the config() method to load the variables. You also need to run the code in dbConnect.js file using require() as follows:

```
const express = require('express');
const morgan = require('morgan');

require('dotenv').config();
require('./libs/dbConnect');
```

The application should be connected to MongoDB cluster now.

You can verify this by looking at the terminal for the 'Connected to MongoDB' log:

```
[nodemon] restarting due to changes...
[nodemon] starting `node index.js`
Connected to MongoDB #<<<<<<
Server running on port 3000
```

And that's how you connect a Node.js application to a MongoDB cluster using Mongoose.

Summary

The code added in this chapter can be found at https://g.codewithnathan.com/node-7

In this chapter, you've seen how to connect the Node application with MongoDB Atlas cluster using Mongoose.

Mongoose is a great library because it provides a schema for our documents, enabling constraints and making sure that the shape of the data is consistent across many documents in one collection.

In the next chapter, we're going to start creating a Mongoose model that will be used in our application.

Chapter 8: Implementing the MVC Pattern

With the MongoDB database connection ready, we can start creating models and use them in our application.

But before we continue with the development process, let's take a minute to understand the MVC design pattern, which we're going to use in the following chapters to build our application.

What's an MVC Pattern?

The MVC pattern is a software development design pattern that divides the related source code into three connected elements.

The **Model** is the definition of the data relevant to the application. This element describes the data structure and the format used to store the data.

The **View** is the visual representation of the application, it's also the interface from which the user can interact with the data in a pleasing and easy manner.

The **Controller** is the main driver of the application. It acts as the bridge between the model and the view.

Here's the MVC pattern that we're going to implement in our Node.js application:

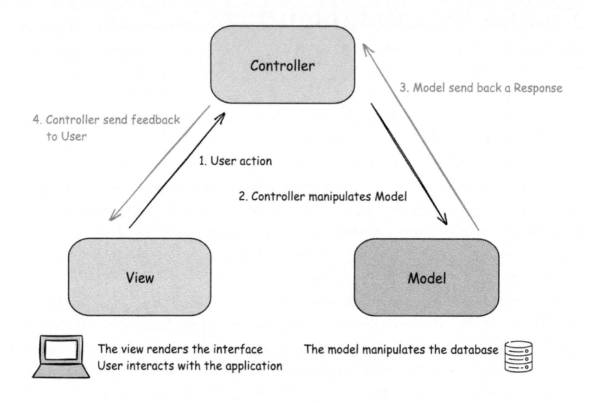

When the user visits our web application, a view will be rendered on the browser.

The user can interact with our application through the view. When the user performs an action, the controller will process that action and fulfill it.

If needed, the controller will access the model to manipulate the database. Once the model returns a response, the controller will process that response and render the right view.

We already created the view layer in our views/ folder, so I will show you how to create the model and controller next.

The first model we're going to create is the User model, which is used for the user authentication process.

We're also going to see how to create a controller that uses the model to interact with the database.

Creating the User Model

Inside the `libs/` folder, create another folder named `models`, then create a file named `user.model.js` inside it.

The content of the `user.model.js` file is as follows. I will explain the code below:

```js
const { Schema, model } = require("mongoose");

const UserSchema = new Schema({
  email: { type: String, required: true, unique: true },
  password: { type: String, required: true },
})

const User = model('User', UserSchema);

module.exports = User;
```

Here, you create a new schema called `UserSchema` that describes the data structure of the User document.

After that, a model is created by calling the `model()` function from `mongoose` library. The first argument serves as the model name, and the second argument is the schema for this model.

A model represents a MongoDB collection, and it's this model that you can use to query documents from the collection.

Before creating the `User` model, we also check if the model already exists under the `models` global. If the model already exists, we reuse that model to avoid creating the model again.

The model is then set as the default export of the file, so any time we need the model, we just need to import it.

Creating User Controller

After creating the User model, you need to create a user controller that will make use of the model.

In the root folder of your project, create a new folder named controllers/, then create a file named user.controller.js in it.

Here's the code you need to write in user.controller.js file:

```javascript
const User = require('../libs/models/user.model');

const createUser = async (req, res) => {
  await User.create({
    email: 'nathan@mail.com',
    password: 'password',
  });

  res.render('user', { message: 'User Created', user: null });
};

const getUser = async (req, res) => {
  const user = await User.findOne({ email: 'nathan@mail.com' });

  res.render('user', { message: 'User Retrieved', user: user });
};

const deleteUser = async (req, res) => {
  await User.findOneAndDelete({ email: 'nathan@mail.com' });

  res.render('user', { message: 'User Deleted', user: null });
};

module.exports = {
  getUser,
  createUser,
  deleteUser,
};
```

In this file, we created three functions: `createUser`, `getUser`, and `deleteUser` to manipulate user data.

Each function will call the right methods from the `User` model that we have created before.

Instead of using the `promise..then` syntax, we use `async/await` operators to make JavaScript wait until the model methods finish running before rendering the view with `res.render()`.

The functions are then exported so that they can be called from the correct route later.

Creating the User View

In the user controller, you can see that the `res.render()` call requires a view called `user`:

```
res.render('user', { message: 'User Retrieved', user: user });
```

We need to create the view layer that will display the `message` and `user` data passed above.

Inside the `views/` folder, create a new file named `user.ejs` and add the code below to it:

```
<!DOCTYPE html>
<html lang="en">
<%- include('./partials/head') %>
<body>
  <div class="m-4">
    <h1 class="text-emerald-500"><%= message %></h1>
    <% if (user) { %>
      <p><%= user.email %></p>
      <p><%= user.password %></p>
```

```
    <% } %>
  </div>
</body>
</html>
```

Here, we copy the view template from `index.ejs` and add a conditional rendering with an `if` statement.

If the `user` data exists, we show the field values, such as the `email` and `password`.

Now we shouldn't show the user password anywhere as it's sensitive, but this is just for showing how to implement the MVC pattern.

We'll update the view in later chapters.

Creating the User Route

Now that we have the model, the view, and the controller for the user data, we need to create routes from which we execute the controller functions.

Back to the root folder of your project, create a new file named `routes/`, then create a file named `user.route.js` that has the following content:

```
const express = require('express');
const router = express.Router();

const {
  getUser,
  createUser,
  deleteUser,
} = require('../controllers/user.controller');

router.get('/', getUser);
router.get('/create', createUser);
router.get('/delete', deleteUser);

module.exports = router;
```

Here, we use the Express router to create three routes, the landing route / will call the getUser() function, the /create route will call the createUser() function, and the /delete route will call the deleteUser() function respectively.

The route is then exported so you can add it to the index.js file.

Open the index.js file, import the user.route.js file and use it as follows:

```
const userRouter = require('./routes/user.route');

const app = express();

// ...

app.get('/', (req, res) => {
  res.render('index', { message: 'Hello From Node.js' });
});

app.use('/users', userRouter);
```

Notice that here we use the app.use() method instead of app.get() because we want to let the userRouter object handle the requests coming to the /users route.

Running the Routes

And now the MVC implementation is completed. If you open the browser and head towards localhost:3000/users/create route, you will see the 'User Created' message.

Now go to localhost:3000/users/ URL and you'll see the user details listed as follows:

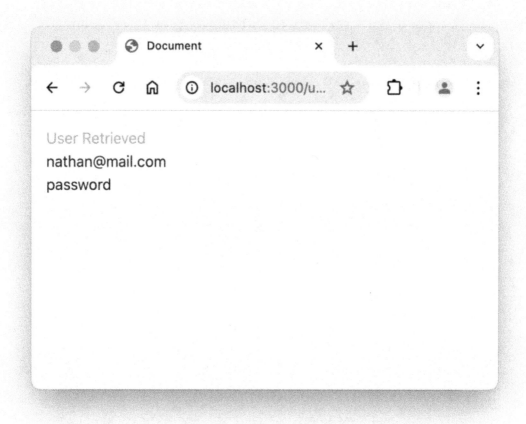

You can also visit MongoDB Atlas and click on Browse collections on the *Overview* page:

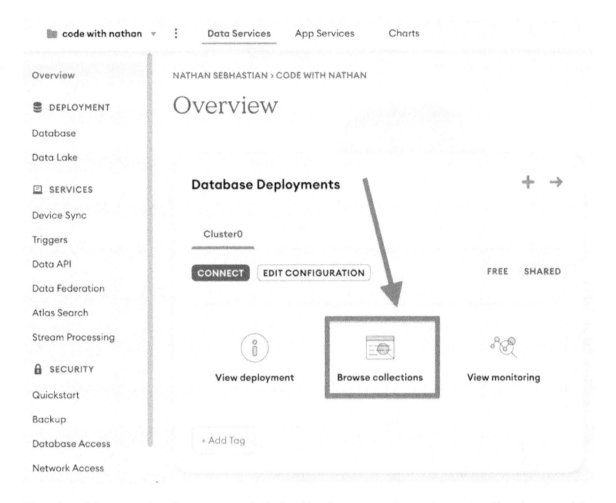

You should see a database named 'finly-db' that contains a 'users' collection, and in that collection, you'll have a document containing your user data:

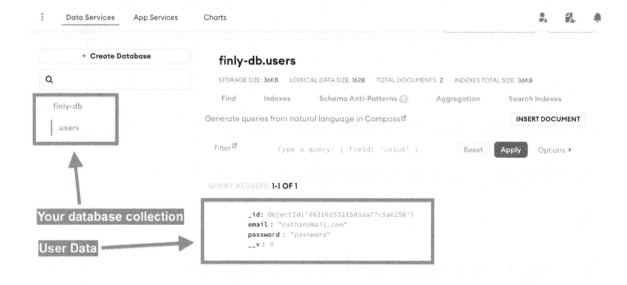

Notice that MongoDB automatically creates the database and collection when you create the first document.

Next, if you visit the `localhost:3000/users/delete` URL from the browser, the user data will be deleted.

This means you've successfully implemented the MVC pattern to develop the user-related actions. Nice work!

Summary

If you need to check the code added in this chapter, you can view the code at https://g.codewithnathan.com/node-8

In this chapter, you've learned how the MVC design pattern can be used in web application development.

Using the MVC pattern enables you to organize your code based on its role in the application. For everything related to the data, we place the code in the model.

For everything related to the interface, we place the code in the view, the rest is stored in the controller. This way, the code is more manageable and scalable.

In the next chapter, we're going to learn how to implement signup and login functionalities to our Express application using the same MVC pattern. I'll see you there.

Chapter 9: Developing User Authentication

With the MVC pattern implemented, the next task is to develop the signup and login process to authenticate the user.

In Express, user authentication can be done by creating a session as an identifier that keeps track of the user.

When the user signs up or logs in to our application, a session is created by Express and sent to the browser as a cookie.

The cookie needs to be included in all subsequent requests sent by the browser. This way, Express knows that the user is allowed to access the resource it wants to access.

When the user logs out, the session and cookie are removed from both the server and the client.

Implementing Express Session

Let's implement the session-based authentication in our Node.js application.

First, you need to install the express-session package using npm:

```
npm install express-session
```

Next, you need to import and use the module in the index.js file as follows:

```
const session = require('express-session');

// ...
```

```
app.use(morgan('dev'));
app.use(express.static('./public'));

app.use(
  session({
    secret: process.env.AUTH_SECRET,
    saveUninitialized: true,
    resave: false,
  })
);
```

We call the `session()` function inside the `app.use()` method, passing three options:

- The `secret` option is the key used to sign the session. It will be used again to verify the cookie later

- The `saveUninitialized` and `resave` options are used to optimize the session storage.

Now we can use the session in our application, but let's add the `AUTH_SECRET` variable in our `.env` file first.

Creating the AUTH_SECRET Variable

The `AUTH_SECRET` is an alphanumeric string that Express uses to sign the session object. You can generate one by using the `openssl` command.

Run the following command from the terminal:

```
openssl rand -base64 32
```

This will generate a string that you can use as the value of `AUTH_SECRET` and put it in the `.env` file.

If your terminal doesn't have `openssl` installed, you can use the one I provide below:

```
AUTH_SECRET=fsfqdB6WAq8TeiT7rRG14afTsZsAYuvJ5/nzWwhmwPw=
```

That will take care of the session signing key. The next step is to create the signup process.

Cleaning The Routes

Before we add the signup process, let's clean the routes we've created on the index.js file first.

Remove the routes for /, /about, and /contact from the application, and leave only the app.use('/') and app.get('*') routes.

When finished, you'll only have two routes as shown below:

```
app.use('/', userRouter);

app.get('*', (req, res) => {
  res.status(404).render('index', { message: 'Not Found' });
});
```

Now open the user.route.js file, remove all routes we've added before, and add new routes for the home page /, /login, and /signup as follows:

```
router.get('/', (req, res) => {
  res.render('pages/index', { title: 'Finly' });
});

router.get('/login', (req, res) => {
  res.render('pages/login', {
    title: 'Sign in',
  });
});

router.get('/signup', (req, res) => {
```

```
    res.render('pages/signup', {
      title: 'Sign up',
    });
  });

  module.exports = router;
```

The next step is to create the sign up page for the view layer.

Creating the Sign Up Page

To better organize our views, create a new folder named pages/ inside the views/ folder.

This folder will keep all pages rendered by our routes.

Next, create a file named signup.ejs and write the code below:

```
<!DOCTYPE html>
<html lang="en">
<%- include('../partials/head') %>
<body>
  <main class="flex mx-auto w-full max-w-[400px] flex-col space-y-2.5 p-4 mt-12">
    <div class="flex h-24 w-full items-end rounded-lg bg-green-500 p-3">
      <div class="flex flex-row items-center text-white">
        <i aria-hidden="true" class="fa-3x fa-solid fa-coins pr-4">
        </i>
        <p class="text-[44px]">Finly</p>
      </div>
    </div>

    <span>
      Already have an account? <a href='/login' class="link link-primary link-hover">Log in</a>
    </span>
  </main>
</body>
</html>
```

This template simply renders the application name and a link to the login page in case the user already has an account

Between the div and span elements, add a form as shown below:

```html
<form action="/signup" method="post" class="space-y-3">
  <div class="flex flex-col rounded-lg bg-slate-100 p-6 gap-4">
    <h1 class="mb-3 text-2xl">Create Your Account Today</h1>
    <label class="input input-bordered flex items-center gap-2">
      <i class="opacity-70 fa-solid fa-envelope">
      </i>
      <input name="email" type="email" class="grow" placeholder="Email" />
    </label>
    <label class="input input-bordered flex items-center gap-2">
      <i class="opacity-70 fa-solid fa-key">
      </i>
      <input name="password" type="password" class="grow" placeholder="Password" />
    </label>
    <label class="input input-bordered flex items-center gap-2">
      <i class="opacity-70 fa-solid fa-key">
      </i>
      <input name="repeatPassword" type="password" class="grow" placeholder="Repeat Password" />
    </label>
  </div>
  <button class="btn btn-primary w-full">
    Sign up
    <i aria-hidden="true" class="ml-auto fa-solid fa-arrow-right fa-lg">
    </i>
  </button>
</form>
```

The sign up form has three inputs: email, password, and repeat password.

Also, note that there are several icons added using the <i> tags. We need to add icon libraries to our application to render those icons.

Adding Font Awesome

We will use Font Awesome to render the icons in our application, so let's add the library to our application.

Inside the `partials/head.ejs` file, add a link to Font Awesome as follows:

```html
<head>
  <title>Document</title>
  <meta charset="UTF-8">
  <meta name="viewport" content="width=device-width, initial-scale=1.0">
  <link href="/styles/style.css" rel="stylesheet" />
  <link
    rel="stylesheet"
    href="https://cdnjs.cloudflare.com/ajax/libs/font-awesome/6.5.1/css/all.min.css"
  />
</head>
```

Also, let's use the `title` dynamic value for the `<title>` tag content as follows:

```html
<title><%= title %></title>
```

This way, the `title` variable from the `res.render()` method call will be used for the value of the `<title>` tag.

Updating User Controller

When the user submits the sign up form, a POST request will be sent to the `/signup` route, so let's create a function in our user controller that will handle the request.

Back to the `user.controller.js` file, delete the `createUser()`, `getUser()`, and `deleteUser()` functions we've added before, then add a new function named `signup()` as shown below:

```js
const signup = async (req, res) => {
  const { email, password } = req.body;
  const query = { email };

  const existingUser = await User.findOne(query);
  if (existingUser) {
```

```
    // Email already exists
    res.redirect('/signup');
  } else {
    const hashedPassword = await bcrypt.hash(password, 10);
    const user = {
      email,
      password: hashedPassword,
    };
    const result = await User.create(user);
    req.session.userId = result._id;
    res.redirect('/dashboard');
  }
};

module.exports = {
  signup,
};
```

This sign up function will take the email and password data from the request body object, and then look for a user with the same email in our database.

If an existingUser is found, we simply redirect to the /signup page.

We need to send a message that says the email is already registered, but we're going to do it later since we need another library for sending the message.

When there's no existingUser, then Express will hash the password value using the bcrypt library.

The hash() function returns a fixed-length alphanumeric characters from the string we passed as its argument.

We haven't installed the bcrypt library used by the signup() function yet, so let's do it now:

```
npm install bcrypt
```

After hashing the password, Express will insert the user data into the database, create a `session` object, and redirect the user to the page.

Adding Express urlencoded Middleware

When handling the POST request, we're going to process form data. Express needs to use the `urlencoded()` middleware to process form data, so let's add it to `index.js` file:

```
app.use(morgan('dev'));
app.use(express.static('./public'));
app.use(express.urlencoded({ extended: false }));
```

The `extended` option is used to let Express know whether we want to process advanced input formats (like nested objects or arrays)

Since we're only going to pass a standard form, we don't need the `extended` option.

Without adding the `urlencoded()` middleware, the form data won't be parsed by Express.

Adding the Dashboard Page

The next step is to create the dashboard page. create a new page in your `views/pages/` folder named `dashboard.ejs` and add the following code:

```
<!DOCTYPE html>
<html lang="en">
<%- include('../partials/head') %>
<body>
  <h1>This is the Dashboard</h1>
</body>
```

Next, create a `dashboard.route.js` file under the `routes/` folder and write the following code:

```
const express = require('express');
const router = express.Router();

router.get('/', (req, res) => {
  res.render('pages/dashboard', { title: 'Dashboard' });
});

module.exports = router;
```

Finally, add the dashboard route into the `index.js` file as follows:

```
const dashboardRouter = require('./routes/dashboard.route');

// ...
app.use('/', userRouter);
app.use('/dashboard', dashboardRouter);
```

Now the `/dashboard` URL is available on your application.

While you can already test the sign up page from the browser, notice that we haven't completed the home page view and apply validation to the sign up page.

Let's take a short break and continue the authentication feature in the next chapter.

Summary

The code added in this chapter can be found at https://g.codewithnathan.com/node-9

In this chapter, you've added the Express session and bcrypt library needed for the authentication process.

You've also created the sign up page for the view and the `signup()` function for the controller.

In the next chapter, we're going to finish the authentication process.

Chapter 10: Validating Form Inputs and Displaying Messages

Currently, we haven't shown an error message when the user already exists, and we also didn't validate the form input values.

This is not right as the user can submit the form without adding any data to it.

To validate form inputs and show error messages we need to use the `express-validator` and `connect-flash` libraries.

I will show you how to integrate both libraries into Express. Let's get started.

Adding Validation to The Sign Up Process

The `express-validator` library is an Express middleware that can be used to validate the `req.body` object values.

Let's install the `express-validator` library using npm:

```
npm install express-validator
```

Next, open the `user.controller.js` file, and add the code below:

```
const { body, validationResult } = require('express-validator');

const validateSignup = [
  body('email', 'Email must not be empty').notEmpty(),
  body('password', 'Password must not be empty').notEmpty(),
  body('password', 'Password must be 6+ characters long').isLength({ min: 6 }),
  body('repeatPassword', 'Repeat Password must not be empty').notEmpty(),
  body('repeatPassword', 'Passwords do not match').custom((value, { req }) => (value ===
req.body.password)),
];
```

The body() function from express-validator gives you access to the body object. In this function, you can pass the property to validate and an error message to send when the validation fails.

Once you select the field, call the validator method to execute on that field, such as notEmpty() and isLength().

Here, we also add a custom() validation function because we want to make sure the value of repeatPassword field is equal to the password field.

This validator array needs to be called before the signup() process, which means we need to export it from the controller:

```
module.exports = {
  signup,
  validateSignup
};
```

And then imports the array inside the user.route.js file as follows:

```
const {
  validateSignup,
  signup,
} = require('../controllers/user.controller');

// ...

router.post('/signup', validateSignup, signup);
```

Back in the user.controller.js file, we can check on the result of the validation inside the signup() method as follows:

```
const signup = async (req, res) => {
  const validationErrors = validationResult(req);
  if (!validationErrors.isEmpty()) {
    const errors = validationErrors.array();
    req.flash('errors', errors);
```

```
      return res.redirect('/signup');
   }

   // ...
}
```

The `validationResult()` returns the `errors` object generated from running the validator functions.

When the `errors` object is not empty, we pass the `errors` as an array to the `flash()` function, then redirect the user to the sign up page.

Now the `flash()` method is a part of the `connect-flash` library, which we haven't added to our application.

We're going to explore this library next.

Storing Error Messages in Flash

The `connect-flash` library provides a special area in the session object called `flash`, which is used for storing messages.

This library is commonly used in combination with redirects so that messages can be passed between requests.

As always, you need to install the library first to use it:

```
npm install connect-flash
```

Next, import and use the module in `index.js` as follows:

```
const flash = require('connect-flash');

// ...
```

```
app.use(flash());
```

Because flash requires an existing session, make sure that you call `app.use(flash())` after `app.use(session())` in your file.

And that's it. Anytime you want to store a message on the flash, you only need to call the `req.flash()` method as shown before:

```
req.flash('key', 'value');
```

The `flash()` method store messages in key-pair values. The first argument is the key you can use to retrieve the message, and the second argument is the value to save.

Displaying Error Messages on Sign Up Form

To retrieve the error messages stored in `flash` object, you need to call the `req.flash()` method and pass the key which stores the message you want to get.

In your `user.route.js` file, add a variable inside the `res.render()` function as follows:

```
router.get('/signup', (req, res) => {
  res.render('pages/signup', {
    title: 'Sign up',
    errors: req.flash('errors'),
  });
});
```

Once a message is retrieved, flash will remove that message from the session.

To display the error messages, you only need to access the `errors` object from EJS template file.

In your `signup.ejs` file, include a partial template below the `<h1>` element as follows:

```
<h1 class="mb-3 text-2xl">Create Your Account Today</h1>
<%- include('../partials/formErrors') %>
```

Next, create the `partials/formErrors.ejs` file and write the following code in it:

```
<% if(typeof errors !== 'undefined') { %>
  <% errors.forEach(function(error) { %>
    <div role="alert" class="alert alert-error">
      <i class="fa-regular fa-circle-xmark"></i>
      <span><%= error.msg %></span>
    </div>
  <% }) %>
<% } %>
```

When the `errors` array is defined, then we iterate over the array using the `forEach()` method and display the `error.msg` string contained in each `error` object.

Now if you try to submit the sign up form without entering any value, you'll get error messages as shown below:

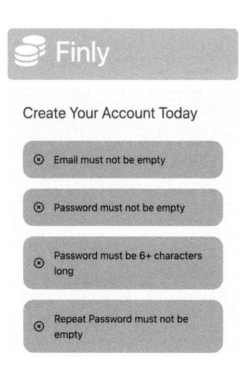

Not only we've displayed the error messages, we've also prevented the the `signup()` function from processing the data further. Nice work!

Preserving Input Data on Sign Up Form

Another thing we need to do is to preserve the input data when the signup process fails.

Right now, the form inputs will be empty after the form fails, and the user needs to re-enter their data into the form.

We can provide a better user experience by keeping the form inputs filled in case of an error.

Back in the `signup()` function in the user controller, add the `req.body` data to the `flash` object as follows:

```
if (!validationErrors.isEmpty()) {
  const errors = validationErrors.array();
  req.flash('errors', errors);
  req.flash('data', req.body);
  return res.redirect('/signup');
}
```

Now we can retrieve user data when rendering the sign up page:

```
router.get('/signup', (req, res) => {
  res.render('pages/signup', {
    title: 'Sign up',
    user: req.flash('data')[0],
    errors: req.flash('errors'),
  });
});
```

With the `user` data retrieved, you can display that data in `signup.ejs` file.

On the `<input>` elements, add a `value` attribute as follows:

```
<input
  name="email"
  type="email"
  class="grow"
  placeholder="Email"
  value="<%= user?.email || '' %>" />

<input
  name="password"
  type="password"
  class="grow"
  placeholder="Password"
  value="<%= user?.password || '' %>" />

<input
  name="repeatPassword"
  type="password"
  class="grow"
  placeholder="Repeat Password"
  value="<%= user?.repeatPassword || '' %>" />
```

Now when the form fails to submit, the error messages will be displayed, and the input values won't be removed.

Showing Toast Notification With Toastify

There's one more part we need to add to the sign up page, and that is to show some notification when the email already exists in our database.

Inside the `signup()` function, we can add another flash message inside the `if (existingUser)` block like this:

```
if (existingUser) {
  req.flash('data', req.body);
  req.flash('info', {
```

```
    message: 'Email is already registered. Try to login instead',
    type: 'error'
  })
  res.redirect('/signup');
}
```

Here, we include the `req.body` to flash to preserve the input values, then we add another flash message under the 'info' key.

When rendering the sign up page, we can add the flash message to a variable as follows:

```
router.get('/signup', (req, res) => {
  res.render('pages/signup', {
    title: 'Sign up',
    user: req.flash('data')[0],
    info: req.flash('info')[0],
    errors: req.flash('errors'),
  });
});
```

Now we need a way to display the `info` data to the user. This is where we need to use a toast notification library called Toastify.

Toastify allows you to show a notification that disappears after a certain time. You can learn more about this library at https://apvarun.github.io/toastify-js

To use this library, you need to add the CSS and JavaScript files to your application.

On the `partials/head.ejs` file, add the CSS part as follows:

```
<link
  rel="stylesheet"
  href="https://cdn.jsdelivr.net/npm/toastify-js/src/toastify.min.css"
/>
```

Next, create a new partial template named `script.ejs` and add the code below:

```
<script type="text/javascript" src="https://cdn.jsdelivr.net/npm/toastify-js"></script>
<% if (typeof info !== 'undefined') { %>
<script>
  const bgColors = {
    error: "#EF4B53",
    success: "#00B5FF"
  }
  Toastify({
    text: ('<%= info.message %>'),
    duration: 3000,
    gravity: 'bottom',
    position: 'right',
    offset: {
      x: 50,
      y: 10
    },
    style: {
      background: bgColors['<%= info.type %>'],
    },
  }).showToast();
</script>
<% } %>
```

Here, we add the link to the JavaScript code for Toastify, then we check if the `info` variable is defined.

When the `info` variable is declared, we create a toast notification by calling the `Toastify()` function and passing the appropriate arguments.

In this case, we want the notification to be positioned at the bottom right, and the background color of the notification would follow the `info.type` value.

Now if you submit the form using an email that's already registered, you should see a toast notification as follows:

After 3000 milliseconds, the notification will disappear.

Let's also show a notification when the user successfully signed up for a new account

On the `else` block where we set the `session.userId` value and redirects to the `/dashboard`, add the following code:

```
else {
  //...
  req.session.userId = result._id;
  req.flash('info', {
    message: 'Signup Successful',
    type: 'success'
```

```
  });
  res.redirect('/dashboard');
}
```

Now the sign up page is completed. We'll continue by adding the login and logout functionalities in the next chapter.

Summary

The code added in this chapter can be found at https://g.codewithnathan.com/node-10

In this chapter, you've learned how to validate user inputs using the `express-validator` library.

After validating the form, you can show any existing error messages by using the `connect-flash` library.

Finally, we also added another feedback in the shape of a toast notification, letting the user know when the email is already registered and when signup is successful.

Chapter 11: Adding Login and Logout Functionalities

Now that the signup process is complete, it's time to add functionalities so users can log in and log out of their existing accounts.

But before we do that, let's improve other parts of the application first, particularly the landing and dashboard page, which we haven't updated for a while

Creating the Landing Page

The landing page is the first page the users will see when they access our application. This page will be a simple introduction page with a single button and an image.

Inside the `views/` folder, you need to create a `pages/index.ejs` file and write the following code:

```
<!DOCTYPE html>
<html lang="en">
<%- include('../partials/head') %>
<body>
  <main class="flex min-h-screen flex-col p-4">
    <div class="flex h-24 shrink-0 items-end rounded-lg bg-green-500 p-4 text-5xl">
      <div class="flex flex-row items-center text-white">
        <i class="fa-solid fa-coins pr-4"></i>
        Finly
      </div>
    </div>
    <div class="mt-4 flex grow flex-col gap-4 md:flex-row">
      <div class="flex flex-col justify-center gap-6 rounded-lg bg-slate-100 px-6 py-10 md:w-2/5 md:px-10">
        <h1 class="text-3xl font-medium">Welcome to Finly!</h1>
        <p class="text-xl text-gray-800">
          The invoicing software for small business and freelancer.
          <br>
          Create professional invoices in an instant with smart invoicing software.
        </p>
        <a class="btn btn-primary w-32" href="/login">
```

```
        Log in
        <i class="ml-auto fa-solid fa-arrow-right"></i>
      </a>
    </div>
    <div class="flex items-center justify-center p-6 md:w-3/5 md:px-20 md:py-8">
      <img alt="Grow your business with Finly" width="400" height="400" src="/images/revenue-bro.png" />
    </div>
  </div>
</main>
<%- include('../partials/script') %>
</body>
</html>
```

You can get the image used in this application at https://g.codewithnathan.com/
revenue-bro.png

In the `dashboard.route.js` file, get the `info` value from flash:

```
router.get('/', (req, res) => {
  res.render('pages/dashboard', {
    title: 'Dashboard',
    info: req.flash('info')[0],
  });
});
```

This flash message will be used when the user logs out later.

Updating the Dashboard Page

Now we need to update the dashboard page. First, create a new partial template
named `navbar.ejs` to create the navigation bar for our application.

This template will have lots of Tailwind classes because it's a custom interface:

```
<div class="fixed w-56 bg-white shadow-md h-screen flex flex-col">
  <div class="h-40 p-4 bg-green-500 text-white text-4xl flex justify-start items-end">
    <i aria-hidden="true" class="fa-solid fa-coins pr-4"></i>
    Finly
  </div>
```

```
<div class="flex grow flex-col py-4 justify-between">
  <ul>
    <li>
      <a href="/dashboard" class="block p-4 hover:bg-sky-100">
        <i aria-hidden="true" class="fa-solid fa-home pr-2"></i>
        Home
      </a>
    </li>
    <li>
      <a href="/dashboard/customers" class="block p-4 hover:bg-sky-100">
        <i aria-hidden="true" class="fa-solid fa-users pr-2"></i>
        Customers
      </a>
    </li>
    <li>
      <a href="/dashboard/invoices" class="block p-4 hover:bg-sky-100">
        <i aria-hidden="true" class="fa-solid fa-copy pr-2"></i>
        Invoices
      </a>
    </li>
  </ul>
  <ul>
    <li>
      <a href="/logout" class="block p-4 hover:bg-sky-100">
        <i aria-hidden="true" class="fa-solid fa-power-off pr-2"></i>
        Sign out
      </a>
    </li>
  </ul>
</div>
</div>
```

Next, add this navigation bar to the dashboard page by updating pages/dashboard.ejs file:

```
<!DOCTYPE html>
<html lang="en">
<%- include('../partials/head') %>
<body class="bg-gray-100">
  <div class="flex h-screen overflow-hidden">
    <%- include('../partials/navbar') %>
    <div class="ml-56 flex-grow p-10 overflow-y-auto">
```

```
        <h1 class=" mb-4 text-xl md:text-2xl">Dashboard</h1>
      </div>
    </div>
  <%- include('../partials/script') %>
  </body>
</html>
```

Now if you visit the dashboard page, you'll see a navigation bar as follows:

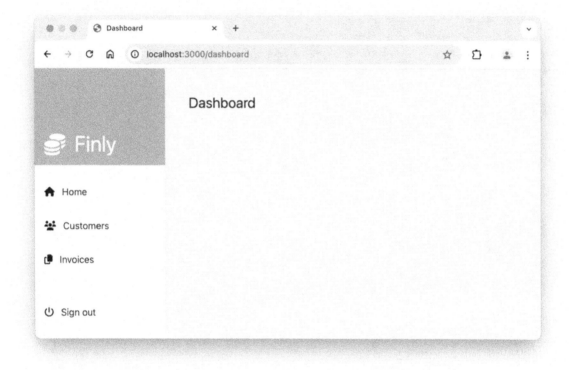

This navigation bar can be used to test the logout function later.

Adding Login Page to Views

To create the login page, you need to add another view file on the pages/ folder.

Create a file named login.ejs and add the code below:

```
<!DOCTYPE html>
<html lang="en">
<%- include('../partials/head') %>
<body>
  <main class="flex mx-auto w-full max-w-[400px] flex-col space-y-2.5 p-4 mt-12">
    <div class="flex h-24 w-full items-end rounded-lg bg-green-500 p-3">
      <div class="flex flex-row items-center text-white">
        <i aria-hidden="true" class="fa-3x fa-solid fa-coins pr-4">
        </i>
        <p class="text-[44px]">Finly</p>
      </div>
    </div>
    <form action="/login" method="post" class="space-y-3">
      <div class="flex flex-col rounded-lg bg-slate-100 p-6 gap-4">
        <h1 class="mb-3 text-2xl">Enter Your Account</h1>
        <%- include('../partials/formErrors') %>
        <label class="input input-bordered flex items-center gap-2">
          <i class="opacity-70 fa-solid fa-envelope">
          </i>
          <input
            name='email'
            type="email"
            class="grow"
            placeholder="Email"
            value="<%= user?.email || '' %>" />
        </label>
        <label class="input input-bordered flex items-center gap-2">
          <i class="opacity-70 fa-solid fa-key">
          </i>
          <input
            name='password'
            type="password"
            class="grow"
            placeholder="Password"
            value="<%= user?.password || '' %>" />
        </label>
      </div>
      <button class="btn btn-primary w-full">
        Log in
        <i aria-hidden="true" class="ml-auto fa-solid fa-arrow-right fa-lg">
        </i>
      </button>
    </form>
    <span>
      Don't have an account? <a href='/signup' class="link link-primary link-hover">Sign Up</a>
    </span>
```

```
    </main>
    <%- include('../partials/script') %>
  </body>
</html>
```

This template file will show a form similar to the sign up form, except it only shows two inputs: email and password.

The next step is to write the controller functions.

Adding Login Function to User Controller

In the `user.controller.js` file, add the `validationLogin` array to validate the login form as follows:

```
const validateLogin = [
  body('email', 'Email must not be empty').notEmpty(),
  body('password', 'Password must not be empty').notEmpty(),
];
```

Next, add the `login()` function as shown below:

```
const login = async (req, res) => {
  const validationErrors = validationResult(req);
  if (!validationFrrors.isEmpty()) {
    const errors = validationErrors.array();
    req.flash('errors', errors);
    req.flash('data', req.body);
    return res.redirect('/login');
  }

  const { email, password } = req.body;
  const user = await User.findOne({ email });
  if (user) {
    const passwordMatch = await bcrypt.compare(password, user.password);
    if (passwordMatch) {
      req.session.userId = user._id;
```

```
          req.flash('info', {
            message: 'Login Successful',
            type: 'success'
          });
          res.redirect('/dashboard');
        } else {
          req.flash('info', {
            message: 'Wrong Password',
            type: 'error'
          });
          req.flash('data', req.body)
          res.redirect('/login');
        }
      } else {
        req.flash('info', {
          message: 'Email is not registered',
          type: 'error'
        });
        req.flash('data', req.body)
        res.redirect('/login');
      }
    }
```

In the code above, the login() function will check on the validation result first, just like the signup() function.

When the form is validated, we will try to find an existing user by using the email value.

When the user is found, we check the password using bcrypt.compare(), then we set the session.userId value to authenticate the user.

If there's any error, we show error messages using flash.

Adding Logout Function

Next, add the logout() function just below the login() function as follows:

```
const logout = (req, res) => {
  req.session.userId = null;
  req.flash('info', {
    message: 'Logout Successful',
    type: 'success'
  });
  res.redirect('/');
};
```

To log out a user, we only need to set the `session.userId` value to `null`, show a flash message indicating that the user is logged out, and redirect to the landing page.

Now we need to export these new functions and validation:

```
module.exports = {
  signup,
  validateSignup,
  login,
  validateLogin,
  logout
};
```

Updating User Routes

The next step is to update the user routes. First, update the imports as shown below:

```
const {
  validateSignup,
  signup,
  validateLogin,
  login,
  logout
} = require('../controllers/user.controller');
```

We need to add a GET and POST routes for the /login URL, and a GET route for the

```
```

/logout URL:

```
router.get('/login', (req, res) => {
  res.render('pages/login', {
    title: 'Sign in',
    user: req.flash('data')[0],
    info: req.flash('info')[0],
    errors: req.flash('errors'),
  });
});

router.post('/login', validateLogin, login);

router.get('/logout', logout);
```

Also, update the landing page to get the info message:

```
router.get('/', (req, res) => {
  res.render('pages/index', {
    title: 'Finly',
    info: req.flash('info')[0],
  });
});
```

The login and logout functionalities are now finished. You can try to log in by navigating to the /login URL from the browser.

Summary

The code added in this chapter is available at https://g.codewithnathan.com/node-11

In this chapter, you've completed the login and logout functionalities, and you've updated the landing page and the dashboard page.

Using the MVC pattern, you set the controller to run database queries using the user model, then show the data by rendering the view.

The MVC pattern organizes our code in a clear way, so we can develop new functionalities faster than when we don't use the pattern.

Chapter 12: Protecting Routes With Middlewares

Now that user authentication is completed, it's time to add a verification process each time the user wants to access a route that requires authentication.

This can be done by using an Express middleware, so let's learn about middleware first.

Express Middleware Explained

In Express, middlewares are functions that have access to the request, response, and next objects.

These objects are defined as `req`, `res`, and `next` in our functions. Express automatically sends these data when it receives an HTTP request.

An Express application is essentially a series of middleware function calls.

The order of the middlewares is determined by the position of `app.use()` function we defined in our `server.js` file.

This is why you need to place your specific routes above general routes like this:

```
app.use('/dashboard', dashboardRouter);

app.use('*', (req, res) => {
  res.status(404).json({ message: 'not found' });
});
```

If you switch the route position like this:

```
app.use('*', (req, res) => {
  res.status(404).json({ message: 'not found' });
});

app.use('/dashboard', dashboardRouter);
```

Then any request will match the * route, so no request will reach the /dashboard route.

Here's a visualization of how Express works:

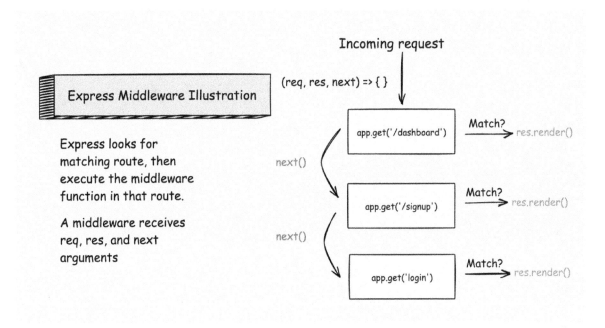

When a request arrives, Express will try to find the middleware that matches the route ordered from top to bottom.

In our application, we use the res.render() method to end the running middleware and send a response back to the browser.

The (req, res, next) parameters are passed to the running middleware automatically.

The next() function can used to run the next middleware. So far, we haven't used this function because we don't need it, but Express always passes this function to all middlewares.

Now that you know what a middleware is, let's create one for protecting our routes.

Adding Verification Middleware

To protect routes from unauthenticated users, you need to create a middleware that verifies the session object that's included in every request.

When this session object contains a valid user id, the request is passed to the next middleware.

If the session isn't valid, then we redirect the user to the login page.

Inside your libs/ folder, create a new file named middleware.js and write the following code in it:

```
const verifyUser = (req, res, next) => {
  if (!req.session.userId) return res.redirect('/login');
  next();
};

module.exports = {
  verifyUser,
};
```

The verifyUser() middleware will check whether there's a valid userId property in the request session object.

When there's no userId property, the function redirects to the login page.

Now you can use this middleware on the dashboard route. Open the index.js file, import the middleware, and place it in the app.use('/dashboard') call as follows:

```
const { verifyUser } = require('./libs/middleware');
```

```
// ...
app.use('/dashboard', verifyUser, dashboardRouter);
```

When unauthenticated users try to access the dashboard page, they will be redirected to the login page.

Creating Middleware to Protect Login and Sign Up Routes

Currently, users can still access the login and sign up pages even after they are authenticated.

To improve the user experience, let's set up a middleware that redirect authenticated users to the dashboard when they access the login or sign up page.

In your middleware.js file, create a new middleware named redirectAuthenticated() as follows:

```
const redirectAuthenticated = (req, res, next) => {
  if (req.session.userId) return res.redirect('/dashboard');
  next();
};

module.exports = {
  verifyUser,
  redirectAuthenticated
};
```

Import the middleware inside the user.route.js file, then place it in front of the sign up and login pages as shown below:

```
const { redirectAuthenticated } = require('../libs/middleware');

router.get('/signup', redirectAuthenticated, (req, res) => {
```

```
    // res.render() ...
});

router.get('/login', redirectAuthenticated, (req, res) => {
    // res.render() ...
});
```

Now whenever authenticated users access the sign up or login page, they will be redirected to the dashboard.

Summary

The code added in this chapter is available at https://g.codewithnathan.com/node-12

In this chapter, you've learned how Express middlewares work and created two middlewares for protecting the routes in your application.

In the next chapter, we're going to develop one of the main features of this application, which is handling customer data.

Chapter 13: Create, Read, Update, and Delete Customers

Now we need to provide a way for users to create, read, update, and delete customers from the application.

Since we've seen the MVC pattern in action before, developing this feature will feel familiar.

We need to start by creating the data model, then create controllers that use request data to manipulate the model accordingly, and then present the data using a view template.

Once the MVC pattern is implemented, we connect it to our application by adding new routes.

Creating the Customer Model

The first thing to do is to create the model. Inside the models/ folder, create a new file named customer.model.js and add the code below:

```
const { Schema, model } = require("mongoose");

const CustomerSchema = new Schema({
  name: { type: String, required: true },
  email: { type: String, required: true, unique: true },
  phone: { type: String, required: true },
  address: { type: String, required: true },
  owner: { type: Schema.Types.ObjectId, ref: 'User' },
})

const Customer = model('Customer', CustomerSchema);
```

```
module.exports = Customer;
```

The model above is connected to the User model through the `owner` field, which reference the `_id` field of the User model.

Now whenever we create a new customer document in MongoDB, we need to provide the `owner` field, or there will be an error.

Creating the Customer Controller

Now we need to create the controller that makes use of the model.

Inside the `controllers/` folder, create the `customer.controller.js` file and begin by importing the model and express validator:

```
const Customer = require('../libs/models/customer.model');

const { body, validationResult } = require('express-validator');
```

Next, create the validation logic for the customer data. Here, we simply check that the values are not empty:

```
const validateCustomer = [
  body('name', 'Name must not be empty').notEmpty(),
  body('email', 'Email must not be empty').notEmpty(),
  body('phone', 'Phone must not be empty').notEmpty(),
  body('address', 'Address must not be empty').notEmpty(),
];
```

Next, we need to create functions to manipulate the user data.

The following `showCustomers()` function will find customers of the current user, then render the customers page:

```
const showCustomers = async (req, res) => {
  const query = { owner: req.session.userId };
  const customers = await Customer.find(query);

  res.render('pages/customers', {
    title: 'Customers',
    type: 'data',
    customers,
    info: req.flash('info')[0],
  });
};
```

You can see here that we use the `req.session.userId` value to find the customers.

Notice there's a new `type` variable added to the `render()` method. This variable will be used by our view template later to show the correct partial template.

The last thing to do is to export the validator and the function:

```
module.exports = {
  showCustomers,
  validateCustomer,
};
```

We'll go back to create more functions later. But for now, let's focus on showing the customer data.

Creating the Customer Views

Let's add the view used by our controller next. Inside the `views/pages/` folder, create a new template named `customers.ejs` with the following content:

```
<!DOCTYPE html>
<html lang="en">
  <%- include('../partials/head') %>
```

```
<body class="bg-gray-100">
  <div class="flex h-screen overflow-hidden">
    <%- include('../partials/navbar') %>
    <div class="ml-56 flex-grow p-10 overflow-y-auto">
      <% if (type === 'data') { %>
        <%- include('../partials/customerData') %>
      <% } else { %>
        <%- include('../partials/customerForm') %>
      <% } %>
    </div>
  </div>
  <%- include('../partials/script') %>
</body>
</html>
```

In this template, we use the `type` variable value to render either the `customerData` or the `customerForm` template.

The `customerData` template will show existing customers along with some buttons to modify the data.

The `customerForm` will render a form to create a new customer or update an existing one.

In your `views/partials/` folder, create the `customerData.ejs` file and write the code below:

```
<div class="w-full">
  <div class="flex w-full items-center justify-between">
    <h1 class="text-2xl"><%= title %></h1>
  </div>
  <form>
    <div class="mt-4 flex items-center justify-between gap-2 md:mt-8">
      <div class="relative flex flex-1 flex-shrink-0">
        <label for="search" class="input input-bordered flex items-center gap-2 w-full">
          <i class="fa-solid fa-magnifying-glass"></i>
          <input id="search" name="search" type="text" class="grow" placeholder="Search customers..." />
        </label>
      </div>
      <a class="btn btn-primary" href="customers/create">
        <i class="fa-solid fa-plus fa-lg mr-2"></i>
        New Customer
```

```
          </a>
        </div>
      </form>
    </div>
```

The above code will render a search input and a button to create a new customer.

Just below the closing </form> tag, add the code to render a table as follows:

```
<div class="mt-6 overflow-x-auto bg-white rounded-lg p-2">
  <table class="table">
    <thead>
      <tr>
        <th>Name</th>
        <th>Email</th>
        <th>Address</th>
        <th>Phone</th>
        <th></th>
      </tr>
    </thead>
    <tbody>
      <% customers.forEach(function(customer){ %>
      <tr>
        <td> <%= customer.name %> </td>
        <td> <%= customer.email %> </td>
        <td> <%= customer.address %> </td>
        <td> <%= customer.phone %> </td>
        <td>
          <div class="flex justify-end gap-3">
            <a class="rounded-md border p-2 hover:bg-gray-100" href="customers/<%= customer._id %>/edit"><i
class="fa-solid fa-pen-to-square fa-lg"></i></a>
            <button class="rounded-md border p-2 hover:bg-gray-100" onclick="deleteModal('<%= customer._id
%>')"><span class="sr-only">Delete</span><i class="fa-solid fa-trash fa-lg"></i></button>
          </div>
        </td>
      </tr>
      <% }); %>
    </tbody>
  </table>
</div>
```

The table above will show the customer data, then show two buttons: one for editing the customer, and one for deleting the customer.

Notice that on the Delete button, there's an onclick attribute that calls the deleteModal() function.

The `deleteModal()` function is used to ask for confirmation from users that they really want to delete the customer data.

First, you need to create a `<dialog>` element that will be used as the modal. You can place this element at the bottom of the template file:

```
<dialog id="delete-modal" class="modal">
  <div class="modal-box">
    <h3 class="font-bold text-lg">Are you sure?</h3>
    <p class="py-4">All invoices related to the customer will be deleted</p>
    <div class="modal-action">
      <form id='delete-form' method="post"><button class="btn btn-danger">Yes</button></form>
      <form method="dialog"><button class="btn">Cancel</button></form>
    </div>
  </div>
</dialog>
```

Next, add a `<script>` element and define the `deleteModal()` function as follows:

```
<script>
  function deleteModal(customerId){
    const modal = document.querySelector('#delete-modal');
    const deleteForm = document.querySelector('#delete-form');
    deleteForm.setAttribute('action', `customers/${customerId}/delete`)
    modal.showModal();
  }
</script>
```

The function simply sets the `action` attribute of the `delete-form` that we created inside the modal, then shows that modal.

When the user clicks on 'Yes', then the customer data will be deleted. Otherwise, the modal is simply disabled again.

Next, you need to create the customer form template. This will be a simple form with four inputs as shown below:

```
<h1 class=" mb-4 text-xl md:text-2xl"><%- title %></h1>
```

```
<form action="<%- formAction %>" method="post">
  <div class="rounded-md bg-slate-100 p-4 md:p-6">
    <div class="flex flex-col gap-4">
      <%- include('../partials/formErrors') %>
      <div class="form-control w-full gap-2"><span class="label-text">Customer Name</span>
        <label for="name" class="input input-bordered flex items-center gap-2">
          <i class="fa-regular fa-user"></i>
          <input id="name" name="name" type="text" class="grow" placeholder="John Doe" value="<%=
customer?.name || '' %>" />
        </label>
      </div>
      <div class="form-control w-full gap-2"><span class="label-text">Email</span>
        <label for="email" class="input input-bordered flex items-center gap-2">
          <i class="fa-regular fa-envelope"></i>
          <input id="email" name="email" type="email" class="grow" placeholder="user@mail.com" value="<%=
customer?.email || '' %>" />
        </label>
      </div>
      <div class="form-control w-full gap-2"><span class="label-text">Phone</span>
        <label for="phone" class="input input-bordered flex items-center gap-2">
          <i class="fa-solid fa-phone"></i>
          <input id="phone" name="phone" type="tel" class="grow" placeholder="+1223456" value="<%=
customer?.phone || '' %>" />
        </label>
      </div>
      <div class="form-control w-full gap-2"><span class="label-text">Address</span>
        <label for="address" class="input input-bordered flex items-center gap-2">
          <i class="fa-regular fa-address-card"></i>
          <input id="address" name="address" type="text" class="grow" placeholder="1 West Pearce St,
Richmond Hill, ON L4B 3K3, Canada" value="<%= customer?.address || '' %>" />
        </label>
      </div>
    </div>
    <div class="mt-6 flex justify-end gap-4">
      <a class="btn btn-ghost" href="/dashboard/customers">Cancel</a>
      <button type="submit" class="btn btn-primary">
        <%= title %>
      </button>
    </div>
  </div>
</form>
```

Now the view is completed. Let's continue with adding the routes.

Creating the Customer Routes

In the routes/ folder, create a customer.route.js file and add the following code:

```
const express = require('express');
const router = express.Router();

const {
  showCustomers,
} = require('../controllers/customer.controller');

router.get('/', showCustomers);

module.exports = router;
```

The customer routes will be nested below the /dashboard route, so you need to import this route on the dashboard.route.js file:

```
const express = require('express');
const router = express.Router();

const customersRouter = require('./customer.route');

// router.get...

router.use('/customers', customersRouter);

module.exports = router;
```

Alright, now you can navigate to the /customers route, but there's only an empty table there for now:

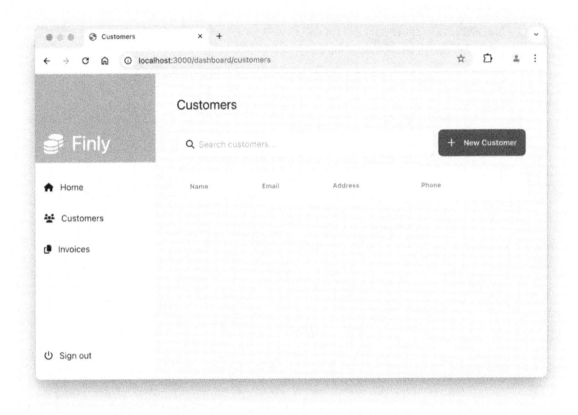

Next, we need to enable the users to create a new customer.

Creating New Customers

Back to the `customer.controller.js` file, add a function to create a customer as follows:

```
const createCustomer = async (req, res) => {
  const validationErrors = validationResult(req);
  if (!validationErrors.isEmpty()) {
    const errors = validationErrors.array();
    req.flash('errors', errors);
    req.flash('data', req.body);
    return res.redirect('create');
  }
}
```

```
    const newCustomer = req.body;
    newCustomer.owner = req.session.userId;

    await Customer.create(newCustomer);
    req.flash('info', {
      message: 'Customer Created',
      type: 'success'
    });
    res.redirect('/dashboard/customers');
  };

  // Update the export module:
  module.exports = {
    showCustomers,
    createCustomer,
    validateCustomer,
  };
```

This function will run after the validator, so it will check on the validation results.

If there's any error, we redirect the user to the create page. Otherwise, we set the newCustomer data and call the Customer.create() method to insert the user to the database.

After that, we simply set the info message and redirect the users to the customers page.

Add Create Routes

Next, add the GET and POST routes to the customer.controller.js file:

```
const {
  showCustomers,
  createCustomer,
  validateCustomer
} = require('../controllers/customer.controller');
```

```
router.get('/', showCustomers);

router.get('/create', function (req, res) {
  res.render('pages/customers', {
    title: 'Create Customer',
    formAction: 'create',
    type: 'form',
    customer: req.flash('data')[0],
    errors: req.flash('errors'),
  });
});

router.post('/create', validateCustomer, createCustomer);
```

Now if you press the '+ New Customer' button on the customers page, you will be shown the customer form:

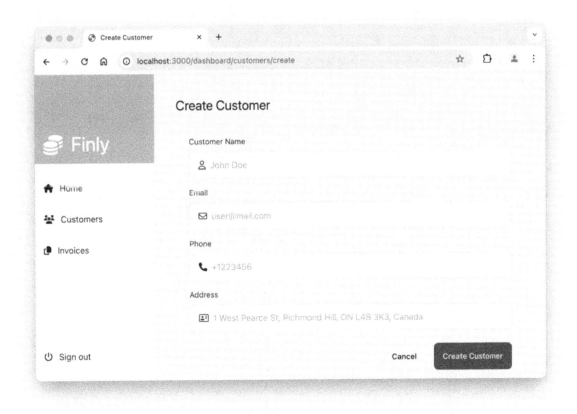

Fill out this form and submit it, and you'll see the customer data shown in the table

Alright, the next step is to update the customers

Updating Existing Customers

In the customer controller, create a function to show existing customer data on the form:

```
const editCustomer = async (req, res) => {
  const customerId = req.params.id;
  const customer = await Customer.findById(customerId);

  res.render('pages/customers', {
    title: 'Edit Customer',
    type: 'form',
    formAction: 'edit',
    customer: req.flash('data')[0] || customer,
    errors: req.flash('errors'),
  });
};
```

This function will be used for the GET route when editing customers.

Next, create a function that will handle the POST route:

```
const updateCustomer = async (req, res) => {
  const validationErrors = validationResult(req);
  if (!validationErrors.isEmpty()) {
    const errors = validationErrors.array();
    req.flash('errors', errors);
    req.flash('data', req.body);
    return res.redirect('edit');
  }

  const customerId = req.params.id;
  const customerData = req.body;

  await Customer.findByIdAndUpdate(customerId, customerData);
```

```
  req.flash('info', {
    message: 'Customer Updated',
    type: 'success'
  });
  res.redirect('/dashboard/customers');
};
```

The function above will call the `Customer.findByIdAndUpdate()` method when the request data passes the validation process.

Also, don't forget to update the module exports content:

```
module.exports = {
  showCustomers,
  editCustomer,
  updateCustomer,
  createCustomer,
  validateCustomer,
};
```

Alright, now you need to create the update routes in `customer.route.js` file:

```
const {
  showCustomers,
  editCustomer,
  updateCustomer,
  createCustomer,
  validateCustomer
} = require('../controllers/customer.controller');

// other routes...

router.get('/:id/edit', editCustomer);

router.post('/:id/edit', validateCustomer, updateCustomer);
```

Now when you click on the edit button, you will be shown a form populated with existing customer data.

You can update the data as you need, then click the submit button to update the database.

Deleting Customers

The last step is to add the delete customer function. This function is very simple:

```
const deleteCustomer = async (req, res) => {
  const customerId = req.params.id

  await Customer.findByIdAndDelete(customerId);
  req.flash('info', {
    message: 'Customer Deleted',
    type: 'success'
  });
  res.redirect('/dashboard/customers');
};

module.exports = {
  showCustomers,
  editCustomer,
  deleteCustomer,
  updateCustomer,
  createCustomer,
  validateCustomer,
};
```

The function will call the findByIdAndDelete() method to delete the customer data.

Next, create the route to delete customers as shown below:

```
const {
  showCustomers,
  editCustomer,
  updateCustomer,
  createCustomer,
  deleteCustomer,
```

```
    validateCustomer
} = require('../controllers/customer.controller');

// ...

router.post('/:id/delete', deleteCustomer);
```

Here, the id of the customer that wants to be deleted will be read from the URL parameter, which we have set in the deleteModal() function.

Now all functionalities relating to the customer data are finished. We still have the search function, which we will add later.

For now, let's take a short break before continuing to the next chapter.

Summary

The code added in this chapter is available at https://g.codewithnathan.com/node-13

In this chapter, you've implemented a new feature to your Node application from scratch.

Here, you used the MVC pattern extensively. First, you create the model, then create the controller function, then the views.

The controller then got connected to the application by creating new routes that call the right controller functions.

Now users can create, read, update, and delete customers. Good work!

Chapter 14: Handling Invoices Data

Now we need to develop a feature to manipulate invoice data, which is the main purpose of our application.

Handling invoice data will be similar to how we handled the customer data in the previous chapter, but there is some extra code for formatting the date and amount values.

Let's begin by creating the model.

Creating the Invoice Model

Inside the models/ folder, create a new file named invoice.model.js and write the code below:

```
const { Schema, model } = require("mongoose");

const InvoiceSchema = new Schema({
  amount: { type: Number, required: true },
  date: { type: String, required: true },
  status: { type: String, required: true },
  owner: { type: Schema.Types.ObjectId, ref: 'User' },
  customer: { type: Schema.Types.ObjectId, ref: 'Customer' },
})

const Invoice = model('Invoice', InvoiceSchema);

module.exports = Invoice;
```

The invoice model is connected to both the user and customer models, so there are owner and customer fields in this model.

Later in the form, we can select the customer that we want to pass the invoice to.

Creating the Invoice Controller

The next step is to create the controller. In the `controllers/` folder, create a new file named `invoice.controller.js` and import the modules that will be used:

```
const Customer = require('../libs/models/customer.model');
const Invoice = require('../libs/models/invoice.model');

const { body, validationResult } = require('express-validator');
```

Next, write the validation logic for the invoice data. Let's just make sure that none of the values are empty:

```
const validateInvoice = [
  body('customer', 'Select the Customer').notEmpty(),
  body('amount', 'Amount must not be empty').notEmpty(),
  body('date', 'Due Date must not be empty').notEmpty(),
  body('status', 'Select the Status').notEmpty(),
]
```

After that, you need to create a function to show the existing invoices.

Let's name it `showInvoices()`:

```
const showInvoices = async (req, res) => {
  const query = { owner: req.session.userId };

  const invoices = await Invoice.find(query);
  res.render('pages/invoices', {
    title: 'Invoices',
    type: 'data',
    invoices,
    info: req.flash('info')[0],
  });
};
```

Now the function to show invoices also needs to retrieve customer data, so you need to use the populate() method from Mongoose.

The populate() method is used to pull referenced document data. Using this method, we can pull the customer name for each invoice we have.

Above the showInvoices() function, create a new function named populateInvoices() as shown below:

```
const populateInvoices = query => {
  return query
  .populate({
    path: 'customer',
    model: Customer,
    select: '_id name',
  })
};
```

The populate method is called on the query object, which is returned when you call the find() method.

This means you can call the populateInvoices() method and pass Invoices.find() as the argument like this:

```
const invoices = await populateInvoices(Invoice.find(query));
```

The customer field will be transformed into an object with _id and name properties.

We'll use this object later in the views. Export the function from the file:

```
module.exports = {
  showInvoices
}
```

Creating the Invoice Views

Now you need to create the invoice views. Create a new template inside the views/pages/ folder named invoices.ejs and add the following content to it:

```
<!DOCTYPE html>
<html lang="en">
  <%- include('../partials/head') %>
  <body class="bg-gray-100">
    <div class="flex h-screen overflow-hidden">
      <%- include('../partials/navbar') %>
      <div class="ml-56 flex-grow p-10 overflow-y-auto">
        <% if (type === 'data') { %>
          <%- include('../partials/invoiceData') %>
        <% } else { %>
          <%- include('../partials/invoiceForm') %>
        <% } %>
      </div>
    </div>
  <%- include('../partials/script') %>
</body>
</html>
```

Now the next step is to create the partial templates.

First, the invoiceData.ejs file. This one is similar to customersData.ejs except for the table content:

```
<div class="w-full">
  <div class="flex w-full items-center justify-between">
    <h1 class="text-2xl"><%= title %></h1>
  </div>
  <form>
    <div class="mt-4 flex items-center justify-between gap-2 md:mt-8">
      <div class="relative flex flex-1 flex-shrink-0">
        <label for="search" class="input input-bordered flex items-center gap-2 w-full">
          <i class="fa-solid fa-magnifying-glass"></i>
          <input id="search" name="search" type="text" class="grow" placeholder="Search invoices..." />
        </label>
```

```
      </div>
      <a class="btn btn-primary" href="invoices/create">
        <i class="fa-solid fa-plus fa-lg mr-2"></i>
        New Invoice
      </a>
    </div>
  </form>
  <div class="mt-6 overflow-x-auto bg-white rounded-lg p-2">
    <table class="table">
      <thead>
        <tr>
          <th>Customer Name</th>
          <th>Amount</th>
          <th>Due Date</th>
          <th>Status</th>
          <th></th>
        </tr>
      </thead>
      <tbody>
        <% invoices.forEach(function(invoice){ %>
        <tr>
          <td> <%= invoice.customer.name %> </td>
          <td> <%= invoice.amount %> </td>
          <td> <%= new Date(invoice.date).toLocaleDateString('en-US') %> </td>
          <td>
            <% if(invoice.status === 'paid') { %>
            <span class="ml-2 badge badge-sm badge-success p-3 gap-3 text-white">
              Paid <i class="fa-regular fa-circle-check"></i>
            </span>
            <% } else { %>
            <span class="ml-2 badge badge-sm badge-ghost p-3 gap-3">
              Pending <i class="fa-regular fa-clock"></i>
            </span>
            <% } %>
          </td>
          <td>
            <div class="flex justify-end gap-3">
              <a
                class="rounded-md border p-2 hover:bg-gray-100"
                href="invoices/<%= invoice._id %>/edit">
                  <i class="fa-solid fa-pen-to-square fa-lg"></i>
              </a>
              <button
                class="rounded-md border p-2 hover:bg-gray-100"
                onclick="deleteModal('<%= invoice._id %>')">
                <span class="sr-only">Delete</span><i class="fa-solid fa-trash fa-lg"></i>
              </button>
            </div>
          </td>
        </tr>
        <% }); %>
```

```
          </tbody>
      </table>
    </div>
  </div>
</div>
<dialog id="delete-modal" class="modal">
  <div class="modal-box">
    <h3 class="font-bold text-lg">Are you sure?</h3>
    <p class="py-4">The invoice will be deleted</p>
    <div class="modal-action">
      <form id='delete-form' method="post">
        <button class="btn btn-danger">Yes</button>
      </form>
      <form method="dialog">
        <button class="btn">Cancel</button>
      </form>
    </div>
  </div>
</dialog>
<script>
  function deleteModal(invoiceId) {
    const modal = document.querySelector('#delete-modal');
    const deleteForm = document.querySelector('#delete-form');
    deleteForm.setAttribute('action', `invoices/${invoiceId}/delete`)
    modal.showModal();
  }
</script>
```

Next, you need to add the invoiceForm.ejs file.

The form will show a datepicker to the users, so we're going to use the vanilla datepicker library available from https://mymth.github.io/vanillajs-datepicker

Open your head.ejs file and add the following CSS library:

```
<link
  rel="stylesheet"
  href="https://cdn.jsdelivr.net/npm/vanillajs-datepicker@1.3.4/dist/css/datepicker.min.css"
/>
```

Now in the partials/ folder, create the invoiceForm.ejs template and write the code below in it:

```
<h1 class=" mb-4 text-xl md:text-2xl"><%- title %></h1>
```

```
<form action="<%- formAction %>" method="post">
  <div class="rounded-md bg-slate-100 p-4 md:p-6">
    <div class="flex flex-col gap-4">
      <%- include('../partials/formErrors') %>
      <div class="form-control w-full gap-2"><span class="label-text">Choose Customer</span>
        <label for="customer" class="input input-bordered flex items-center gap-2">
          <i class="fa-regular fa-user"></i>
          <select class="grow cursor-pointer" name="customer" id="customer">
            <option value="">Select Customer</option>
            <% customers.forEach(function(customer){ %>
            <option value="<%= customer._id %>"
              <%= String(invoice?.customer?._id) === String(customer._id) ? 'selected' : '' %>>
              <%= customer.name %>
            </option>
            <% }) %>
          </select>
        </label>
      </div>
      <div class="form-control w-full gap-2"><span class="label-text">Amount</span>
        <label for="amount" class="input input-bordered flex items-center gap-2">
          <i class="fa-solid fa-dollar-sign"></i>
          <input id="amount" name="amount" type="number" class="grow" placeholder="Enter in USD" value="<%=
invoice?.amount || '' %>" />
        </label>
      </div>
      <div class="form-control w-full gap-2"><span class="label-text">Due Date</span>
        <label for="date" class="input input-bordered flex items-center gap-2">
          <i class="fa-regular fa-calendar"></i>
          <input id="date" name="date" type="text" class="grow" placeholder="4/5/2024" value="<%=
invoice?.date? new Date(invoice.date).toLocaleDateString('en-US') : '' %>" />
        </label>
      </div>
      <div class="form-control w-full gap-2"><span class="label-text">Status</span>
        <div for="status" class="input input-bordered flex items-center gap-2">
          <div class="flex gap-4">
            <div class="flex items-center">
              <input type="radio" name="status" id="pending" class="radio" value="pending" <%= invoice
?.status === 'pending' ? 'checked' : '' %> />
              <label for="pending" class="ml-2 badge badge-sm badge-ghost p-3 gap-3">Pending <i class="fa-
regular fa-clock"></i></label>
            </div>
            <div class="flex items-center">
              <input type="radio" name="status" id="paid" class="radio" value="paid" <%= invoice?.status
=== 'paid' ? 'checked' : '' %> />
              <label for="paid" class="ml-2 badge badge-sm badge-success p-3 gap-3 text-white">Paid <i
class="fa-regular fa-circle-check"></i></label>
            </div>
          </div>
        </div>
      </div>
    </div>
    <div class="mt-6 flex justify-end gap-4">
```

```
      <a class="btn btn-ghost" href="/dashboard/invoices">Cancel</a><button type="submit" class="btn btn-
  primary">
        <%= title %>
      </button>
    </div>
</form>
```

The form contains a select input for the customer, a number input for the amount, a datepicker for the due date, and a radio input for the status.

Next, you need to add the scripts to render the datepicker:

```
<script
  src="https://cdn.jsdelivr.net/npm/vanillajs-datepicker@1.3.4/dist/js/datepicker-full.min.js">
</script>
<script>
  const elem = document.querySelector('#date');
  const datepicker = new Datepicker(elem, {
    autohide: true,
    format: 'm/d/yyyy'
  });
</script>
```

Here, the datepicker is rendered on the #date element, which is the invoice due date input we've added above.

Creating the Invoice Route

The next step is to create the invoice route file. You already know the pattern here.

Inside the routes/ folder, create an invoice.route.js file and write the code below:

```
const express = require('express');
const router = express.Router();

const {
  showInvoices,
} = require('../controllers/invoice.controller');
```

```
router.get('/', showInvoices);

module.exports = router;
```

Then, import route in dashboard.route.js:

```
const invoicesRouter = require('./invoice.route');

// ...
router.use('/invoices', invoicesRouter);
```

Now you can already visit the /dashboard/invoices URL from the browser, but there's only an empty table there.

Create New Invoices

Next, go back to the invoice.controller.js and add the createInvoice() function:

```
const createInvoice = async (req, res) => {
  const validationErrors = validationResult(req);
  if (!validationErrors.isEmpty()) {
    const errors = validationErrors.array();
    req.flash('errors', errors);
    req.flash('data', req.body);
    return res.redirect('create');
  }

  const newInvoice = req.body;
  newInvoice.owner = req.session.userId;

  await Invoice.create(newInvoice);
  req.flash('info', {
    message: 'New Invoice Created',
    type: 'success'
  });
  res.redirect('/dashboard/invoices');
```

```
};
```

Oh and since we need to get the customer data for the invoice form, let's create another function to get the customer data:

```
const getCustomers = async (req, res, next) => {
  const customersQuery = { owner: req.session.userId };
  const customers = await Customer.find(customersQuery);
  req.customers = customers;
  next();
};
```

The customers data is attached to the req.customers property, so the next middleware can access the data there.

Export the functions from the file:

```
module.exports = {
  showInvoices,
  createInvoice,
  getCustomers,
  validateInvoice
};
```

And add the routes for creating new invoices in invoice.route.js:

```
const {
  showInvoices,
  createInvoice,
  getCustomers,
  validateInvoice
} = require('../controllers/invoice.controller');

router.get('/create', getCustomers, (req, res) => {
  const { customers } = req;
  res.render('pages/invoices', {
    title: 'Create Invoice',
```

```
      formAction: 'create',
      type: 'form',
      customers,
      invoice: req.flash('data')[0],
      errors: req.flash('errors'),
    });
  });


  router.post('/create', validateInvoice, createInvoice);
```

Notice that the `getCustomers()` function are called on the GET route. This is so that we can use the data when rendering the form.

Update Invoices

The next step is to enable updating invoices. Back on the `invoice.controller.js` again, write the `editInvoice()` function:

```
const editInvoice = async (req, res) => {
  const invoiceId = req.params.id;
  const invoice = await populateInvoices(Invoice.findById(invoiceId));
  const { customers } = req;

  res.render('pages/invoices', {
    title: 'Edit Invoice',
    type: 'form',
    formAction: 'edit',
    customers,
    invoice: req.flash('data')[0] || invoice,
    errors: req.flash('errors'),
  });
};
```

This will populate the existing invoice data on the form.

Next, create the `updateInvoice()` function:

```
const updateInvoice = async (req, res) => {
  const validationErrors = validationResult(req);
  if (!validationErrors.isEmpty()) {
    const errors = validationErrors.array();
    req.flash('errors', errors);
    req.flash('data', req.body);
    return res.redirect('edit');
  }

  const invoiceId = req.params.id;
  const data = req.body;

  await Invoice.findByIdAndUpdate(invoiceId, data)
  req.flash('info', {
    message: 'Invoice Updated',
    type: 'sucess'
  });
  res.redirect('/dashboard/invoices');
};
```

Don't forget to update the exports too:

```
module.exports = {
  showInvoices,
  createInvoice,
  getCustomers,
  editInvoice,
  updateInvoice,
  validateInvoice
};
```

Next, create the routes for updating the invoice in invoice.route.js:

```
const {
  showInvoices,
  createInvoice,
  editInvoice,
  updateInvoice,
  getCustomers,
```

```
   validateInvoice
} = require('../controllers/invoice.controller');

router.get('/:id/edit', getCustomers, editInvoice);

router.post('/:id/edit', validateInvoice, updateInvoice);
```

And done! Now you can update existing invoices.

Delete Invoices

The last step is to enable the delete invoice function.

Again, back to the controller:

```
const deleteInvoice = async (req, res) => {
  const invoiceId = req.params.id

  await Invoice.findByIdAndDelete(invoiceId);
  req.flash('info', {
    message: 'Invoice Deleted',
    type: 'success'
  });
  res.redirect('/dashboard/invoices');
};

module.exports = {
  showInvoices,
  editInvoice,
  deleteInvoice,
  updateInvoice,
  createInvoice,
  getCustomers,
  validateInvoice
};
```

Then create the route:

```
const {
  showInvoices,
  editInvoice,
  createInvoice,
  updateInvoice,
  deleteInvoice,
  getCustomers,
  validateInvoice
} = require('../controllers/invoice.controller');

//...

router.post('/:id/delete', deleteInvoice);
```

And that's it. Now you can manipulate the invoice data as required.

Delete All Invoices When a Customer is Deleted

Since the invoices are connected to a single customer, let's delete all invoices for the same customer.

Open your customer.controller.js file, import the invoice model, and update the deleteCustomer() function:

```
const Invoice = require('../libs/models/invoice.model');

const deleteCustomer = async (req, res) => {
  const customerId = req.params.id

  // delete invoices by that customer
  await Invoice.deleteMany({customer: customerId});
  await Customer.findByIdAndDelete(customerId);
  req.flash('info', {
    message: 'Customer Deleted',
    type: 'success'
  });
  res.redirect('/dashboard/customers');
```

```
};
```

This way, the customer and invoice data will always be up to date.

Summary

The code added in this chapter is available at https://g.codewithnathan.com/node-14

In this chapter, you've implemented a feature to create, read, update, and delete invoices from the application.

Aside from a few small differences like rendering a datepicker and creating a select input, the invoice views are similar to the customer views.

The application is almost finished. You did a great job!

Chapter 15: Using Chart.js On the Dashboard

Right now, our dashboard is still empty, so let's fill it with customer and invoice data to show some insights.

We will also use Chart.js to draw a chart on the dashboard showing the revenue in the last 6 months.

Formatting the Currency

Before we code the dashboard page, let's fix a little issue from the previous chapter.

When you open the invoices page, notice that the invoice amount is shown as is:

Customer Name	Amount	Due Date	Status
jonius dora	150	4/26/2024	Pending ○
Zendaya	200	4/30/2024	Pending ○
Randy Winston	300	2/15/2024	Paid ⊘
Lola	100	2/1/2024	Paid ⊘
jonius dora	50	3/20/2024	Paid ⊘

To make it more pleasing, let's format the amount in USD instead of just bare numbers.

In the `libs/` folder, create a new file named `formatter.js` and add the code below:

```
const USDollar = new Intl.NumberFormat('en-US', {
  style: 'currency',
  currency: 'USD',
});

module.exports = {
  USDollar,
};
```

The code above creates a new international number format object that can be used to format numbers.

Now in the `invoice.controller.js` file, import the object and pass it to the `res.render()` method that renders the invoice table:

```
const { USDollar } = require('../libs/formatter');

// ...
const showInvoices = async (req, res) => {
  const query = { owner: req.session.userId };

  const invoices = await populateInvoices(Invoice.find(query));
  res.render('pages/invoices', {
    title: 'Invoices',
    type: 'data',
    invoices,
    USDollar, //  <<<<<
    info: req.flash('info')[0],
  });
};
```

After passing the object, you can use it in the `invoiceData.ejs` file as follows:

```
<td> <%= USDollar.format(invoice.amount) %> </td>
```

Now if you open the invoices page, you see the number formatted as $300.00. Looks nice!

Creating the Dashboard Controller

The dashboard page of the application will show several important insights to the user.

First, there are 4 boxes showing the total sum of invoices that have been paid, are still pending, total invoices created, and total customers:

Dashboard

💵 Collected	🕐 Pending	📁 Total Invoices	👥 Total Customers
$450.00	$350.00	5	4

Because the dashboard doesn't create new data, we don't need a model.

In the `controllers/` folder, create a new file named `dashboard.controller.js` and write the code below:

```
const Customer = require('../libs/models/customer.model');
const Invoice = require('../libs/models/invoice.model');

const { USDollar } = require('../libs/formatter');

const showDashboard = async (req, res) => {
  // ...
}
```

```
module.exports = {
  showDashboard,
};
```

The showDashboard() function needs to get the data required by the dashboard page.

Inside the function, get the total count of the customers and invoices using the countDocument() method first:

```
const query = { owner: req.session.userId };

const invoiceCount = await Invoice.countDocuments(query);
const customerCount = await Customer.countDocuments(query);
```

Next, you need to get all invoices created by the user, then pull the customer name using populate() like this:

```
const allInvoices = await Invoice.find(query)
.populate({
  path: 'customer',
  model: Customer,
  select: '_id name',
});
```

The above code will fetch all invoice data. You can then use the reduce() JavaScript function to get the total amount of paid and pending invoices:

```
const totalPaid = allInvoices.reduce((sum, invoice) => {
  return invoice.status === 'paid' ? sum + invoice.amount : sum;
}, 0);

const totalPending = allInvoices.reduce((sum, invoice) => {
  return invoice.status === 'pending' ? sum + invoice.amount : sum;
}, 0);
```

Now call the res.render() method to render the view:

```
res.render('pages/dashboard', {
  title: 'Dashboard',
  invoiceCount,
  customerCount,
  totalPaid,
  totalPending,
  USDollar,
  info: req.flash('info')[0]
});
```

Updating the Dashboard View

With the controller completed, it's time to add the 4 boxes to the view template.

Update the pages/dashboard.ejs template as shown below:

```
<!DOCTYPE html>
<html lang="en">
<%- include('../partials/head') %>
<body class="bg-gray-100">
  <div class="flex h-screen overflow-hidden">
    <%- include('../partials/navbar') %>
    <div class="ml-56 flex-grow p-10 overflow-y-auto">
      <h1 class=" mb-4 text-2xl"><%= title %></h1>
      <div class="grid gap 6 sm:grid-cols-2 lg:grid-cols-4">
        <div class="rounded-xl bg-white p-2 shadow-sm">
          <div class="flex p-4">
            <i aria-hidden="true" class="fa-solid fa-money-bills"></i>
            <h3 class="ml-2 text-sm font-medium">Collected</h3>
          </div>
          <p class=" truncate rounded-xl border-slate-200 border px-4 py-8 text-center text-2xl">
            <%= USDollar.format(totalPaid) %>
          </p>
        </div>
        <div class="rounded-xl bg-white p-2 shadow-sm">
          <div class="flex p-4">
            <i aria-hidden="true" class="fa-regular fa-clock"></i>
            <h3 class="ml-2 text-sm font-medium">Pending</h3>
          </div>
          <p class=" truncate rounded-xl border-slate-200 border px-4 py-8 text-center text-2xl">
            <%= USDollar.format(totalPending) %>
```

```
        </p>
      </div>
      <div class="rounded-xl bg-white p--2 shadow-sm">
        <div class="flex p-4">
          <i aria-hidden="true" class="fa-regular fa-folder-open"></i>
          <h3 class="ml-2 text-sm font-medium">Total Invoices</h3>
        </div>
        <p class=" truncate rounded-xl border-slate-200 border px-4 py-8 text-center text-2xl">
          <%= invoiceCount %>
        </p>
      </div>
      <div class="rounded-xl bg-white p--2 shadow-sm">
        <div class="flex p-4">
          <i aria-hidden="true" class="fa-solid fa-users"></i>
          <h3 class="ml-2 text-sm font-medium">Total Customers</h3>
        </div>
        <p class=" truncate rounded-xl border-slate-200 border px-4 py-8 text-center text-2xl">
          <%= customerCount %>
        </p>
      </div>
    </div>
  </div>
  </div>
  <%- include('../partials/script') %>
</body>
</html>
```

The code above uses CSS grid to make the layout of the 4 boxes responsive.

Now if you open the dashboard page, you will see the insights shown.

Showing the Revenue Chart

Below the 4 boxes, we're going to add a revenue chart that shows the revenue for the last 6 months.

We're going to use Chart.js to do this, and if you never use Chart.js before, don't worry because it's quite simple to use.

Basically, Chart.js allows you to create a chart on top of the HTML <canvas> element by calling a function and specifying the options for the chart.

Back in the `dashboard.ejs` file, you can create an empty `<canvas>` element below the `<div>` with `grid` class as follows:

```
<!-- <div class="grid gap-6 sm:grid-cols-2 lg:grid-cols-4"> -->
<div class="mt-6 grid grid-cols-1 gap-6 md:grid-cols-4 lg:grid-cols-8">
  <div class="w-full md:col-span-4">
    <h2 class=" mb-4 text-2xl">
      Recent Revenue
    </h2>
    <div class="rounded-xl bg-white p-4">
      <canvas id="revenueChart" width="600" height="400"></canvas>
      <div class="flex items-center pb-2 pt-6">
        <i aria-hidden="true" class="fa-regular fa-calendar fa-lg"></i>
        <h3 class="ml-2 text-sm text-slate-1000">Last 6 months</h3>
      </div>
    </div>
  </div>
</div>
```

Now we can render the chart on the `revenueChart` canvas.

At the bottom of the file, add a link to fetch Chart.js code, then create a new chart instance by calling the `new Chart()` function:

```
<script src="https://cdn.jsdelivr.net/npm/chart.js"></script>
<script>
  const canvas = document.getElementById('revenueChart');
  Chart(canvas, {
    type: 'bar',
    data: {
      labels: ['Red', 'Blue', 'Yellow', 'Green', 'Purple', 'Orange'],
      datasets: [{
        label: 'Revenue',
        data: [100, 200, 300, 400, 500, 600],
        backgroundColor: 'rgba(75, 192, 192, 0.2)',
        borderColor: 'rgba(75, 192, 192, 1)',
        borderWidth: 1
      }]
    },
    options: {
```

```
      scales: {
        y: {
          beginAtZero: true
        }
      }
    }
  });
</script>
```

When you call the `new Chart()` function, pass the canvas as the first argument, and the chart options as the second argument.

Here, we pass the `type` of the chart we want to render, which is the bar chart.

The `data` object allows you to specify the data to use in the chart. The `labels` here will label each bar generated.

The `datasets` property contains various options, but the most important one is the `data` array, which is the value represented by the chart.

The above script will generate the following chart:

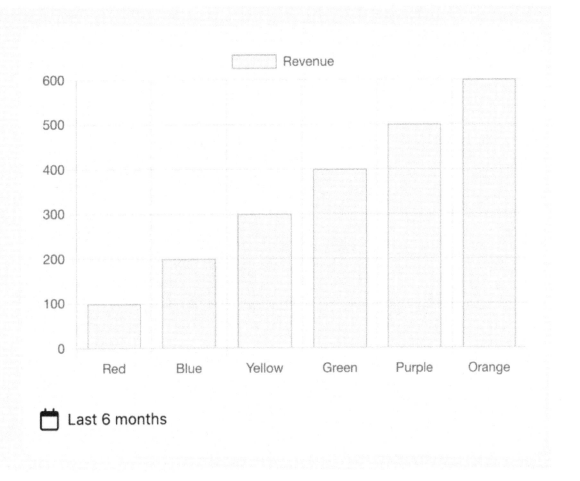

To make the chart represent our invoice data, we only need to adjust the `labels` and `data` array.

Back in the `invoice.controller.js` file, update the `showDashboard()` function with the following code:

```
const revenueData = [];

for (let i = 0; i < 6; i++) {
  const today = new Date();
  today.setMonth(today.getMonth() - i);
  const firstDay = new Date(today.getFullYear(), today.getMonth(), 1);
  const lastDay = new Date(today.getFullYear(), today.getMonth() + 1, 0);
  const month = today.toLocaleString('default', { month: 'short' });
```

```
    const revenueForMonth = allInvoices
      .filter(invoice => {
        return (
          new Date(invoice.date) >= firstDay &&
          new Date(invoice.date) <= lastDay
        );
      })
      .reduce((total, invoice) => total + invoice.amount, 0);

    revenueData.unshift({ month, revenue: revenueForMonth });
  }
```

The code looks a bit complicated, but the main point is that the for loop will run 6 times, and in each loop, we get the revenue data for a month.

The loop begins in the current month, and then moves backward for the last 6 months.

As a result, the revenueData variable becomes an array of objects that contain the name of the month and the revenue for that month like this:

```
[
  { month: 'Nov', revenue: 300 },
  { month: 'Dec', revenue: 100 },
  { month: 'Jan', revenue: 0 },
  { month: 'Feb', revenue: 400 },
  { month: 'Mar', revenue: 50 },
  { month: 'Apr', revenue: 350 }
]
```

Next, pass the revenueData to the dashboard page as a JSON string in res.render():

```
res.render('pages/dashboard', {
  title: 'Dashboard',
  revenueData: JSON.stringify(revenueData),
  // ...
});
```

Now you can use the `revenueData` variable on the `<script>` tag for rendering the chart:

```
<script>
  const revenueData = JSON.parse('<%- revenueData %>');
  const canvas = document.getElementById('revenueChart');
  new Chart(canvas, {
    type: 'bar',
    data: {
      labels: revenueData.map(item => item.month),
      datasets: [{
        label: 'Revenue',
        data: revenueData.map(item => item.revenue),
        backgroundColor: 'rgba(75, 192, 192, 0.2)',
        borderColor: 'rgba(75, 192, 192, 1)',
        borderWidth: 1
      }]
    },
    // ...
  });
</script>
```

The `revenueData` is parsed using the `JSON.parse()` method, then the values are passed to the `labels` and `data` options using the array `map()` method.

Now if you refresh the dashboard page, your invoice data will be reflected on the chart:

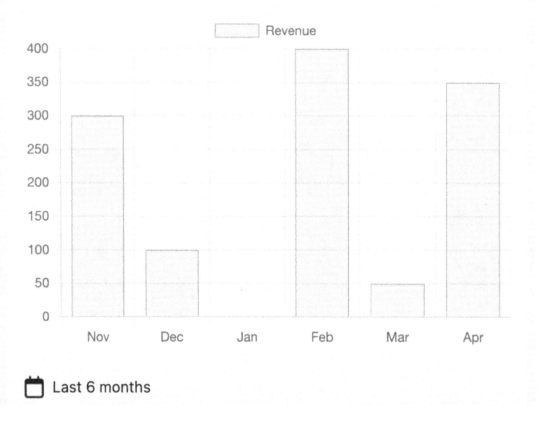

Recent Revenue

Last 6 months

In my application, I didn't create any invoice in January, so it's shown as empty.

Showing Five Latest Invoices

The last part of the dashboard page will show the customer name, amount, and status of 5 latest invoices.

In the dashboard controller, you need to sort the `allInvoices` data in descending order, then slice the first 5 elements of the array as follows:

```
allInvoices.sort((a, b) => new Date(b.date) - new Date(a.date));
```

```
const latestInvoices = allInvoices.slice(0, 5);
```

Now pass the latestInvoices data to the view:

```
res.render('pages/dashboard', {
  title: 'Dashboard',
  latestInvoices,
  // ...
});
```

And update the view template to render the invoices as shown below:

```
<!-- <div class="w-full md:col-span-4"> -->
<div class="flex w-full flex-col md:col-span-4">
  <h2 class=" mb-4 text-2xl">
    Latest Invoices
  </h2>
  <div class="flex grow flex-col justify-between rounded-xl bg-white p-4">
    <div class="border-slate-200 border px-6">
      <% latestInvoices.forEach(invoice => { %>
      <div class="flex flex-row items-center justify-between py-4">
        <div class="flex items-center">
          <p class="truncate font-semibold text-base">
            <%= invoice.customer.name %>
          </p>
          <p class="hidden text-sm text-slate-1000 sm:block">
            <% if(invoice.status === 'paid') { %>
            <span class="ml-2 badge badge-sm badge-success p-3 gap-3 text-white">
              Paid <i class="fa-regular fa-circle-check"></i>
            </span>
            <% } else { %>
            <span class="ml-2 badge badge-sm badge-ghost p-3 gap-3">
              Pending <i class="fa-regular fa-clock"></i>
            </span>
            <% } %>
          </p>
        </div>
        <p class=" truncate font-medium">
          <%= USDollar.format(invoice.amount) %>
```

```
      </p>
    </div>
    <% }) %>
  </div>
  <div class="flex items-center pb-2 pt--6">
    <i aria-hidden="true" class="fa-regular fa-note-sticky fa-lg"></i>
    <h3 class="ml-2 text-sm text-slate-1000">Last 5 invoices</h3>
  </div>
  </div>
</div>
```

And that's it. Now you should be able to see the last 5 invoices as shown below:

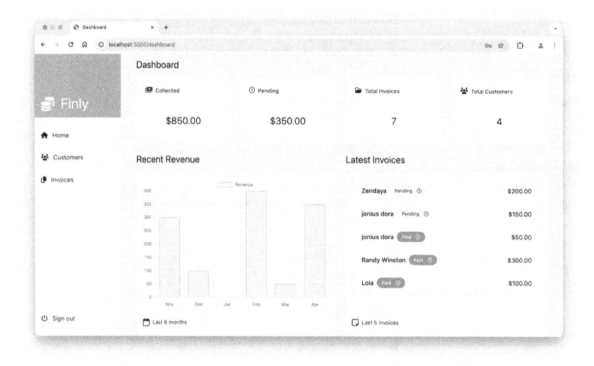

The dashboard page is now complete. Well done!

Summary

The code added in this chapter is available at https://g.codewithnathan.com/node-15

In this chapter, you've learned how to format numbers using the international number format in JavaScript.

You've also updated the dashboard page to show some insights to the user, displaying the total amount of collected and pending invoices, and adding Chart.js to show the revenue chart.

You've come a very long way! Only one more chapter, then we can deploy this application for others to see.

Chapter 16: Adding the Search Feature

With the dashboard page done, the last feature to develop is the search feature on the customer and invoice pages.

If you type something into the search bar and then press Enter, you will see that the input value is already added to the URL query parameter under the ?search= parameter:

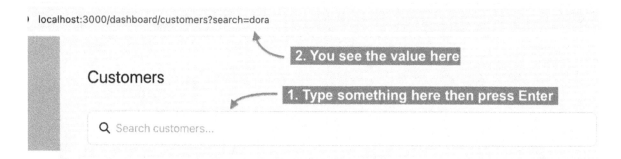

This means that the view is already reacting to the user action. You only need to update the controller to take into account the search value and filter the returned results.

Adding Customer Search

Let's do the customer search first. In the showCustomers() function, get the search query parameter from the req.query object as follows:

```
const query = { owner: req.session.userId };

const { search } = req.query;
if (search) {
  query['$or'] = [
    { name: { $regex: search, $options: 'i' } },
    { email: { $regex: search, $options: 'i' } },
    { phone: { $regex: search, $options: 'i' } },
```

```
      { address: { $regex: search, $options: 'i' } },
  ]
};
```

When the search variable is defined, we add the $or operator so that Mongoose will search for any matching value in the name, email, phone, and address fields.

The rest of the code stays the same, so if you do a search now, you will see only matching customer data on the table.

Adding Invoice Search

The next step is to add a search function to the invoice. We need to make the invoice searchable using the customer's name.

In the showInvoices() function, unpack the search value from req.query object, then pass it to the populateInvoices() function as follows:

```
const { search } = req.query;

const invoices = await populateInvoices(Invoice.find(query), search);
```

The next step is to update the populateInvoices() function. You need to add the match option when the search argument is defined.

To make this possible, separate the options passed to the populate option as a variable, then modify the populate option only when search is defined:

```
const populateInvoices = (query, search) => {
  const populateOptions = {
    path: 'customer',
    model: Customer,
    select: '_id name',
  };
  if (search) {
```

```
      populateOptions['match'] = { name: { $regex: search, $options: 'i' } };
   }
};
```

The customer property will be null when the customer data doesn't match the search value, so you need to filter the invoice data and remove all invoices that have the customer value of null.

This can be done on the return statement, where you can chain the populate() method call with a then() as follows:

```
return query
  .populate(populateOptions)
  .then(invoices => invoices.filter(invoices => invoices.customer != null));
```

Alright, now the invoices can be filtered by the customer name field.

Summary

The code added in this chapter can be found at https://g.codewithnathan.com/node-16

Here, you just added the controller functions to process the search query parameter passed by the views.

Mongoose can filter the data you want to retrieve by using the $or operator.

When you need to filter a populated field, you can add the match option, and then remove all documents that don't have a matching result.

Chapter 17: Deploying Node.js Application

The Finly invoicing application is now finished.

All that's left is to deploy the application to a production server so that you can show your work to others.

Preparing the Application for Deployment

Before deploying the application let's clean some files that are no longer used.

In the `views/` folder, you can see that we still have the `index.ejs` and `user.ejs` files that are used in the beginning.

The `user.ejs` file is no longer used, so it can be deleted.

The `index.ejs` file is still used for the wild card route * to display the 'Not Found' message, so let's clean up the content of the file.

Remove the paragraph and the button from the template, then add class to style the `<h1>` tag as follows:

```
<!DOCTYPE html>
<html lang="en">
<%- include('./partials/head') %>
<body>
  <h1 class="text-2xl m-5"><%= message %></h1>
</body>
</html>
```

Next, open the `index.js` file to update the * route and add the `title` variable:

```
app.get('*', (req, res) => {
  res.status(404).render('index', {
    title:'Not Found',
    message: 'Not Found'
  });
});
```

Also, we need to duplicate the devcss command but omit the watch -w option. Let's call the command css as follows:

```
{
  "css": "postcss public/styles/tailwind.css -o public/styles/style.css",
  "devcss": "postcss public/styles/tailwind.css -o public/styles/style.css -w"
}
```

This is because we're not going to watch for any changes after deploying the application.

Pushing Code to GitHub

Deploying an application requires you to grant access to the project files and folders. GitHub is a platform that you can use to host and share your software project.

Head over to https://github.com/ and login or register for a new account if you don't have one already.

From the dashboard, create a new repository by clicking + New on the left sidebar, or the + sign on the right side of the navigation bar:

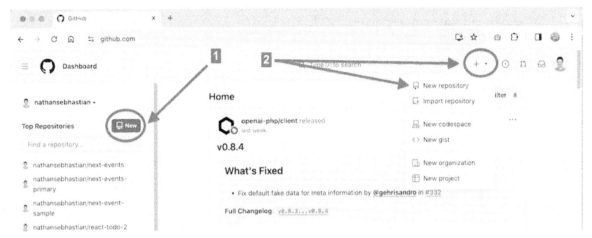

Figure 11. Two Ways To Create a Repository in GitHub

A repository (or repo) is a storage space used to store software project files.

In the *Create a Repository* page, fill in the details of your project. The only required detail is the repository name:

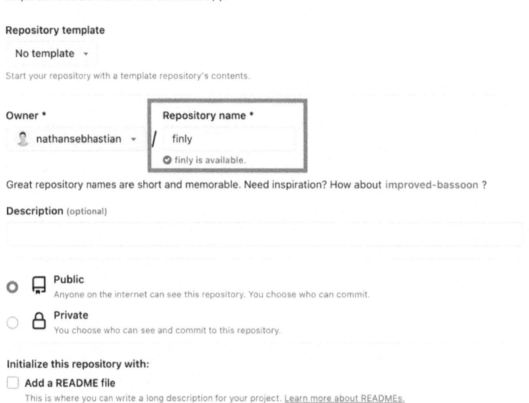

You can make the repository public if you want this project as a part of your portfolio, or you can make it private.

Once a new repo is created, you will be given instructions on how to push your files into the repository.

You need to follow the instruction for pushing an existing repo:

...or push an existing repository from the command line

```
git remote add origin https://github.com/nathansebhastian/taskly-client.git
git branch —M main
git push —u origin main
```

Figure 12. How to Push Existing Repo to GitHub

Now you need to create a repository for your project. Open the command line on the finly/ folder, then run the git init command:

```
git init
```

This will turn your project into a local repository. Add all project files into this local repo by running the git add . command:

```
git add .
```

Changes added to the repo aren't permanent until you run the git commit command. Commit the changes as shown below:

```
git commit -m 'Ready for Deployment'
```

The -m option is used to add a message for the commit. Usually, you summarize the changes committed to the repository as the message.

Now you need to push this existing repository to GitHub. You can do so by following the GitHub instructions:

```
git remote add origin <URL>
git branch -M main
git push -u origin main
```

You might be asked to enter your GitHub username and password when running the git push command.

Once the push is complete, refresh the GitHub repo page on the browser, and you should see your project files and folders there.

This means our application is already pushed (uploaded) to a remote repository hosted on GitHub.

The remote server where we're going to deploy our application can fetch the code from this repository.

Deploying Node Application to Railway

Railway is a cloud platform that you can use for building and deploying a web application.

The platform offers a free tier that you can use to deploy the Node application we've created.

You can sign up for an account at https://railway.app and agree to the privacy policy and fair use agreement.

Here are the next instructions:

1. Click on *Create New Project* to start deploying your application.
2. Select *Deploy from GitHub repo*
3. Select *Configure GitHub App* and allow Railway to access your repos
4. After enabling access, you will be taken back to the Railway page
5. Select the Taskly server repo to deploy it.
6. Click on + *Add variables*

Railway will deploy your application, and you'll be taken into the Variables setting.

Here, you need to click on the *Raw Editor* link to open a text editor. Open your `.env` file, then copy and paste it to the Railway editor.

Click Save or Update Variables and see the variables we have recorded as follows:

Railway should automatically redeploy the application for you.

The next step is to run the `css` command that we've added in the build process.

On the Railway menu, click the *Settings* page, and type 'build command' into the filter input. You should see the *Custom Build Command* option.

Click the + *Build Command* button, then enter `npm run css`:

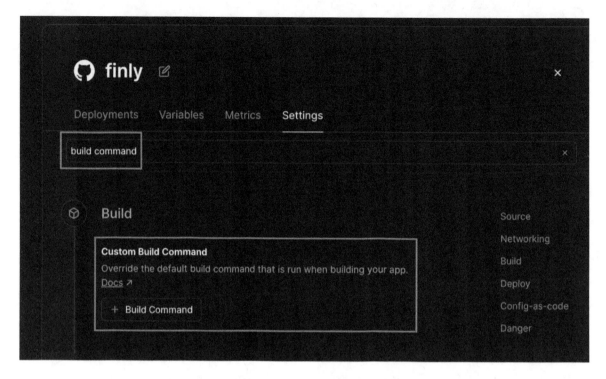

Save the changes, and Railway will ask for your permission to deploy the changes.

Next, we need to enable HTTP access by generating a domain name.

Still on the *Settings* page type 'domain' into the filter input to see the *Public Networking* option.

Click the *Generate Domain* button as shown below:

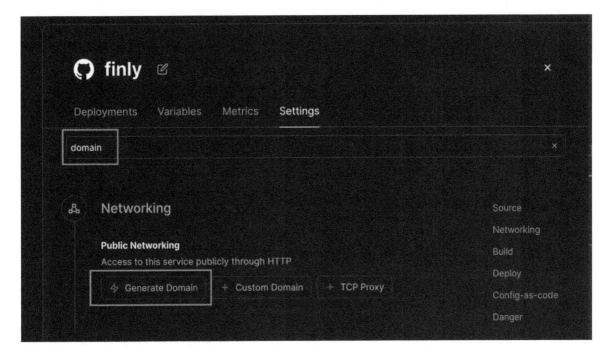

Railway will assign a domain for your application and enable access from that domain URL.

With that, the deployment is completed. You can try to access the application using the given domain.

Summary

The code changes up to this chapter is available at https://g.codewithnathan.com/node-17

In this chapter, we clean up the project code a little before we deploy the application to the public internet.

We also created a GitHub repository to store our code as the source for the deployment, and finally deployed the Node.js application on Railway.

It's time to give yourself a pat on the back because you just passed a very important milestone in your knowledge gain. I'm so proud of you!

Wrapping Up

Congratulations on finishing this book! It wasn't easy, but you did it anyway.

You have learned how to use Node.js to build a complex full-stack web application, and then deploy it to production.

I hope you enjoyed learning and exploring Node.js with this book as much as I enjoyed writing it.

I'd like to ask you for a small favor.

If you enjoyed the book, I'd be very grateful if you would leave an honest review on Amazon (I read all reviews coming my way)

Every single review counts, and your support makes a big difference.

Thank you and all the best for your career in tech!

Until next time,

Nathan

About the author

Nathan Sebhastian is a senior software developer with 8+ years of experience in developing web and mobile applications.

He is passionate about making technology education accessible for everyone and has taught online since 2018.

www.ingramcontent.com/pod-product-compliance
Lightning Source LLC
LaVergne TN
LVHW081343050326
832903LV00024B/1283